DESIGN CROCHET

Contents

DESIGN CROCHET

Library of Congress Catalog Card Number: 78–53417

ISBN: 0–8015–2019–3

1 2 3 4 5 6 7 8 9 10

DESIGN CROCHET

Lillian Bailey
Linda Osborne Blood
Nan Jennes Brown
Judith Copeland
Del Pitt Feldman
Jacqueline Henderson
Arlene Mintzer
Barbara Muccio

edited by Mark Dittrick
photographs by Jeffrey Fox

HAWTHORN BOOKS, INC.
Publishers/NEW YORK
A Howard & Wyndham Company

List of Abbreviations

arnd = around

att = attach

beg = begin

ch = chain

cont = continue

dc(s) = double crochet(s)

dec = decrease

dtrc = double treble crochet

ea = each

hdc = half double crochet

hk = hook

inc = increase

lp(s) = loop(s)

p(s) = picot(s)

patt = pattern

rem = remaining

rep = repeat

rnd(s) = round(s)

sc(s) = single crochet(s)

sk = skip

sl lp = slip loop

sl st = slip stitch

sm sp = same space

sp(s) = space(s)

st(s) = stitch(es)

tog = together

tr = triple

trc = triple crochet

wrh = wool around hook

yo = yarn over

Yarns noted in instructions are given generically. Unusual or special yarns and the addresses of their manufacturers or distributors are given in the back of the book.

I

Preface

Design Crochet is a very special book, and what makes it so special goes beyond the fact that never before have so many imaginative and beautiful crochet designs been collected between the covers of a single volume. *Design Crochet* is a first. Eight of America's most talented and best-known professional crochet designers have joined together to create their own book and, especially for it, a collection of original, inspired designs that have never been seen or published previously. Lillian Bailey, Linda Osborne Blood, Nan Jennes Brown, Judith Copeland, Del Pitt Feldman, Jacqueline Henderson, Arlene Mintzer, and Barbara Muccio are the contributors. Having them all together in one exciting book is truly a major event in the world of crochet.

And *Design Crochet* is unique for other reasons. The instructions printed here, all carefully checked for accuracy, are presented just as each designer wrote them—the way they are submitted to the magazine editors and yarn company fashion directors. So, in addition to step-by-step directions, many of the instructions contain the designer's own comments, helpful notes and hints—personal touches seldom found in a magazine or crochet pamphlet. And there's something different about the projects, too. When working for a magazine or yarn company, a designer is almost always required to use the yarns of only one manufacturer or importer, a restriction that obviously limits creative freedom. In *Design Crochet* there are no such requirements, and the results speak for themselves.

In *Design Crochet*, these eight truly outstanding names of crochet design share with us their thoughts about their craft and how they go about the business of creating garments and objects that set the standard for crochet in America. I invite you to share in their event. I am proud to be a part of it.

Mark Dittrick

DESIGN CROCHET

Lillian Bailey

Thousands of crochet enthusiasts have already "met" Lillian Bailey—in a special story about her and her work in the fall/ winter 1977 issue of Ladies' Home Journal Needle & Craft. Since her first appearance in that magazine in 1974, hardly an issue has come out without one or more of her designs inside. Lillian Bailey-designed garments have also appeared in Good House- keeping magazine, Good Housekeeping Needlecraft, Family Cir- cle Fashions & Crafts, Woman's Day Needlework Ideas, and American Home Crafts. In addition to being one of the top cro- chet designers around, Lillian, a graduate of Boston's Massachu- setts College of Art, is an accomplished painter, silk screen designer, embroiderer, frame-loom weaver, needlepointer, and punch hooker. And she's even done some package designing.

"Sometimes I have to live with a yarn for a while before I get a clear idea of what I ought to do with it. I'll have the yarn in a wide range of colors sitting in a pile in my workroom, and every so often I'll move the colors around, take a few away, put some back, switch one for another. When three or four colors are right and the idea for what to do with them starts to come, I know it. It all starts with the yarn.

"Where you buy yarn is important. I buy yarn where I'm confident the people in the store know something about their merchandise. If you buy where the people are unfamiliar with their stock, their answers to questions you might have could lead you in the wrong direction. In a good yarn store you're likely to find shoppers who really know their crocheting. You will learn more than you can imagine by talking to an experienced craftsperson. I'm always happy to talk crochet with someone in a yarn shop and exchange a hint or two—such as how to rip out mohair or a loop yarn without getting it all snarled. I don't know why it works, but I've discovered that by holding the crochet in such a way that I gently pull down to rip out rather than up, I get far fewer snags. That's not the sort of thing you're likely to discover on your own, but it is something a talkative crochet designer might tell you while standing in front of a bin of mohair."

Lillian Bailey

Mohair Pastel Blouson

Size:

Directions are for sizes Medium and Large. For Small size, see directions.

Materials:

1 Spool chainette rayon yarn (Lavender)
Rose brushed wool (A)   7 skeins (2 oz. each)
Yellow-Orange brushed wool (B)   2 skeins (2 oz. each)
Beige brushed wool (C)   2 skeins (2 oz. each)
Lavender brushed wool (D)   1 skein   (2 oz.)
Natural brushed wool (E)   1 skein   (2 oz.)

Hook:

Size J aluminum or size to obtain gauge.

Gauge:

3 patterns = 2¼″, 4 rows = 2″.

Finished measurement = 20″ across back.

Note: Read all instructions before starting.

BACK:

Ch 63 with color A (Small size ch 52). Work 1 row sc.

Row 1: Ch 1, turn. 1 Sc, 1 dc across, ending with dc (pattern st). Ch 1, turn.

Rows 2 and 3: Rep Row 1.

Row 4: Work for 4″. Att B, work to end of row. Ch 1, turn.

Row 5: Work across row. Att C. Ch 1, turn.

Rows 6, 7, and 8: Work in C. Ch 1, turn.

Row 9: Work for 8″. Att D, work to end of row. Ch 1, turn.

Row 10: Work in D for 8″. Att B, complete row. Ch 1, turn.

Row 11: Work B to last 2″. Att E, complete row. Ch 1, turn.

Row 12: Work in E across row. Att B, ch 1, turn.

Row 13: Work across row. Att A, ch 1, turn.

Rows 14 and 15: Work in A, ch 1, turn.

Row 16: Work to 10″ from end. Att D, complete row. Ch 1, turn.

Row 17: Work 4″ with D. Att C, complete row. Ch 1, turn.

Rows 18 and 19: Work across row. Att B, ch 1, turn.

Row 20: Work across row. Ch 1, turn.

Row 21: Work 9″. Att E, complete row. Ch 1, turn.

Row 22: Work across row. Att A, ch 1, turn.

Rows 23 and 24: Work in A. Ch 1, turn.

Row 25: Work 11″. Att D, complete row. Ch 1, turn.

Row 26: Work 6″. Att C, finish row. Ch 1, turn.

Rows 27 and 28: Work in C, ch 1, turn.

Row 29: Work 5″. Att B, (carry along C) and work to within 5″ from end, drop B, and tie off. Pick up C and finish row. Ch 1, turn.

Row 30: (This is right side of garment.) Work row of C, att A, ch 1, turn.

Row 31: Work in A for 3 rows, or 15″ from beg.

BACK ARMHOLES:

Row 1: Sl st in ea of first 4 sts. Ch 1 (do not turn), work in pattern to within last 4 sts. *Do not work last 4 sts.* Ch 1, turn.

Row 2: Draw up a lp in ea of first 2 sts. (Draw up a lp in first st as for a sc, yo hook and draw up a lp in next st as for a dc, yo and through 2 lps, yo and through 3 lps.) One st dec made. Cont across in pattern to last 2 sts and dec 1 st as before. Rep last row three times more (46 sts). Now work in pattern on these sts until armhole measures 9″ (deep armhole). End off.

FRONT:

Work same as back through 19th row. Ch 1, turn. Work for 5″. Att B (carry along C), and work to within 5″ from end, drop B, pick up C, and cont to end. Att A, ch 1, turn.

Row 20: Work across row for 9″. Att E, complete row. Ch 1, turn.

Row 21: Work across row. Att A, ch 1, turn.

Row 22: Work across row. Att B, ch 1, turn.

Row 23: Work over 8″. Att A (carry along B), and work to within 8″, pick up B, carry along A, and finish row. Pick up A, ch 1, turn. Tie off B.

Row 24: Work across row. Ch 1, turn.

Row 25: Work across row. Att C, ch 1, turn.

Rows 26, 27, and 28: Work across rows. Att A, ch 1, turn.

Row 29: Work across row. Ch 1, turn.

NECK AND FRONT ARMHOLES:

Mark center st of row.

Row 1: Work in pattern to 2 sts before center st. Dec 1 st. * *Do not work over remaining sts.* Ch 1, turn.

Row 2: Work across row. Ch 1, turn.

Row 3: Work across row and dec 1 st at end of row. Rep last 2 rows once more. Shape armhole as on back. Work from * and at the same time cont to dec at neck as before until you have worked 3 armhole dec, then cont to dec at neckline but work even at armhole edge until 9″ from start of armhole (19 rows). Break off and fasten. Go back to center front. Skip marked st, att yarn to next st, ch 1. Work dec over first 2 sts. Work in pattern across. Complete neck and armhole to correspond with other side.

BACK NECKBAND:

Skip first 4″ (or 11 sts) for shoulder. Att A in 12th st and sc in same st and in every st to within 4″ of other shoulder (or 12 sts from end). *Do not work over remaining sts.* Drop A, att B, ch 1, turn, dec 1 sc at beg of row, sc in ea sc to last 2 sc. Ch 1, turn. Work 1 more row B following color sequence (see below).

FRONT NECKBAND:

Att A to bottom of V on right neck edge. Sc along edge in the end of rows (careful to keep edge flat and even) to shoulder. Ch 1, turn. Sc in ea st to last 2 sc. Dec 1 st. Ch 1, turn. Work rows in color sequence. Dec every 2nd row at lower edge. Rep for left neckband using color sequence below.

Color sequence: 2 rows B, 2 rows C, 1 row chainette, 2 rows A.

SLEEVES:

Ch 55 A. Work 1 row sc, then 2 rows in pattern st.

Row 4: Work for 6″. Att B, complete row. Ch 1, turn.

Row 5: Work across row. Att C, ch 1, turn.

Rows 6, 7, and 8: Work across row. Ch 1, turn.

Row 9: Work for 8″. Att D, complete row. Ch 1, turn.

Row 10: Work for 6″. Att B, complete row. Ch 1, turn.

Row 11: Work to within 2″ from end. Att E, complete row. Ch 1, turn.

Row 12: Work across row. Att B, ch 1, turn.

Row 13: Work across row. Att A, ch 1, turn.

Rows 14 and 15: Work across rows. Ch 1, turn.

Row 16: Work for 12″. Att D, complete row. Ch 1, turn.

Row 17: Work for 4″. Att C, complete row.

Now work the same as back through Row 22, ch 1, turn. Work 2 rows in pattern with A, then att B, and working in sc rep neckband stripe. Then go back to working in pattern for 10 rows or 17″. Work *one more row even, then a dec on next row. Rep from * twice more. Work one row even and end off.

FINISHING:

Sew shoulder seams and back and front neckband seams, matching rows. Sew center front neckband, right over left and left over right on wrong side. Sew side and sleeve seams and sew in sleeves.
Work row of sc around bottom of sleeves with A. Work second row. Dec in ea st. Work third row. Dec every other st or whatever is needed to fit cuff.
For cuffs ch 23 in chainette, work sc in back lps for as many rows as needed to fit wrist comfortably, then close seams. Sew cuffs to sleeve.
Work row of sc around bottom of sweater with A. Ch 2, turn, work row of dc, then row of sc. Fold this row up to first sc row on wrong side for casing. Make ch with double strand of A 60″ long. Thread through casing.

Impressionist Garden Coat

Size:

Directions fit sizes Small and Medium. For Large size, work chain 6″ longer for back and simply divide in half for each front. This is a midi-length coat. To shorten, eliminate one or two rows of Fur St pattern in colors A and B at bottom of coat. (Example: 1 row of A and 1 row of B.) Measure length of sleeve and adjust as needed. Width of sleeve here is 19″ (for deep armhole).

Materials:

Brushed variegated yarn 77 percent wool, 23 percent viscose—2-oz. skeins.

Green (A)	20 skeins
Lavender (B)	4 skeins
Scarlet (C)	3 skeins
Pink (D)	2 skeins
Yellow-Orange (E)	2 skeins

½″ Velvet cord 6 yds. in color to match outside of coat; 2nd color if desired.

Hook:

Size J aluminum or size to obtain gauge. Size H aluminum for finishing.

Gauge:

6 dc = 2″. Distance between Fur St rows = 1½″.

Note: Fur Stitch: Work row of sc. Ch 1, turn, 1 sc in back lp of first sc, ch 5, * 1 sc in next sc, ch 5. Rep from * across row, ending ch 5; 1 sc in last sc. Ch 1, turn. Holding lps down in front facing you, sc in *back* lps of last row to end. Turning chains count as 1 st. Count sts every few rows.

Read all instructions before starting.

BACK:

Ch 77 to measure 30″ with A.

Row 1: 1 Sc in 2nd ch from hook and in ea ch to end (76 sts). Ch 2, turn.

Row 2: Dc across row. Ch 1, turn.

Row 3: Work Fur St in back lps of sts across row. Ch 1, turn.

Row 4: Work sc in rem lp of dc of last row across. Ch 2, turn.

Row 5: Dc across row. Ch 1, turn.

Row 6: Sc across row. Ch 1, turn.

Rep from Row 3 six times (7 Fur St rows).

At the end of this section att B and rep pattern from Row 3 five times. Work *only* Fur St rows in color B. All sc and dc rows are worked in main color A throughout the coat. The color change is made only on Fur St rows with some exceptions.

At the end of this section drop B and att color C. Work as before three times (3 Fur St rows).

At the end of this section att color D and work 1 row Fur St. Work A rows as usual, then work Fur St row in B.

Always remembering to work background (right side of coat) with A, continue changing colors on Fur St rows as follows: 1 Fur St row C, 1 row D, 1 row A (this is an exception), 1 row B, 1 row C, 1 row D. Next repeat Fur St rows in colors * A, B, C, then 1 row E, then Fur St row D.

Rep from * once more at the end of Fur St row D, att A, ch 1, turn. Work row of sc, ch 1, turn. At end of row cont with A. Ch 1, turn. All color A background rows will be worked in sc from here on. Now work 2 rows sc, 1 row Fur St, 1 row sc, all in A. Ch 1, turn. Sc across on 29 sts (for shoulder), ch 1, turn, work another row sc. Break off. Att yarn in 29th st from other shoulder (right side of back). Ch 1 and work 2 rows sc on these 29 sts.

FRONTS:

Make two. Ch 40 to measure 17″. 1 Sc in 2nd ch from hook and in ea ch across (39 sts).

Left and right fronts are worked the same as back on these 39 sts until the last Fur St A row is reached.

On this row (for left front) work Fur St on 29 sc of row below, ch 1, turn, sc on these 29 sts. Ch 1, turn. Work 3 rows sc. End off.

For right front, complete sc row before last Fur St row. End off. Turn. Att A in the 11th st. Ch 1, work Fur St on rem sts. Ch 1, turn. Work sc (in back lps) across. Ch 1, turn. Work 3 rows sc. End off.

Make two. Ch 50 with A loosely to measure approx 20″. Sc across row. Ch 2, turn, dc across row, ch 1, sc across row, ch 1, turn, work Fur St in back lps across row, ch 2, turn, dc across row. Ch 1, turn, sc across row. Drop A, att B, ch 1, turn.

Work in pattern using this color sequence in Fur St rows B, C, E, D—1 row Fur St of those colors three times or to the desired length of sleeve.

After last Fur St row work 1 row sc in back lps, then work 2 rows sc. End off.

POCKETS:

With A ch 22.
Row 1: Ch 1 in 2nd ch from hook and in ea ch across. Ch 1, turn.
Rows 2 and 3: Sc across. Ch 2, turn.
Row 4: Dc in ea sc across. Ch 2, turn.
Rep Rows 2 through 4 three times.

Sew pockets on at desired height about 3″ in from center opening.

FINISHING:

With H hook and one strand of A, sl st shoulder seams tog. With right sides together line up sleeves between next to last A Fur St rows on front and back (18″ armhole). Sew to body of coat. Sew side seams together on wrong (fur) side of coat. *On right side*, with A work a row of sc around neckline and down front of coat. Work sc into next to last dc and over last dc to prevent hole. Work 2nd row of sc around neckline dec at shoulders and dec 1 st between center back and shoulder, dec 1 st at center back and dec 1 st between center back and other shoulder.

Cut enough cording to go around neckline and down both center fronts and a little extra. Start at bottom of front opening from wrong side. Hold cording parallel to sc row and work sc st over cording all along fronts and neckline (tack cording at beginning and end to prevent shifting). At neckline work 3 sc in corner sc. Tack bottom corners of fronts to wrong side to prevent curling.

Take 3 strands of remaining cording starting 15″ from end and begin braiding 3 strands together for about 14″. Sew beginning and end of braid to prevent ravelling. Mark center of braid and pin to center back of neckline. Sew firmly. There will be about 2″ on each end of neckline free. Knot ends of braid.

Donegal Tweed Suit

Sizes:

Jacket directions are for Small (8 to 10). Directions for Medium (12 to 14) and Large (16 to 18) are in parentheses.

Materials:

Amounts of yarn are listed first.

Donegal tweed wool yarn—bulky weight and worsted weight, 4-oz. skeins.

Bulky:

Charcoal	8 skeins
Dark Brown	3 skeins
Medium Brown	1 skein

Worsted:

Lavender	1 skein
Grape	1 skein
Dusty Rose	1 skein
Beige	1 skein

Brushed wool variegated yarn—2-oz. skeins.

Almond	3 skeins
Sand	1 skein

Skirt elastic, 1″ wide	1 yd.
Matching grosgrain ribbon, 1½″ wide	1 yd.

The following are the yarn combinations I have used:
- Charcoal bulky (A)
- Medium Brown bulky (B)
- Beige worsted and Almond brushed wool, 2 tog (C)
- Lavender worsted and Sand brushed wool, 2 tog (D)
- Lavender worsted and Grape worsted, 2 tog (E)
- Dusty Rose worsted, 2 tog (F)
- Charcoal Brown bulky (G)
- Lavender worsted and Beige worsted (H)
- Dusty Rose worsted and Almond brushed wool (I)
- Almond brushed wool, 2 tog (J)
- Grape, 2 tog (K)

Hook:

Size J aluminum or size to obtain gauge.

Gauge:

3 dc = 1″; 4 rows dc = 3″.

Note: Many of these worsted-weight yarns are used in combinations of two strands held together. It would be helpful to roll each skein of worsted-weight yarn into two balls. The bulky-weight yarn is used singly. The brushed wool comes in a pull skein so there is no need to roll it into a ball. Read all instructions before starting.

JACKET:

The jacket body is worked in color sequence as follows: 8 rows dc A, 1 row dc B, 1 row dc C, 1 row dc D, 1 row dc E, 1 row dc B, 2 rows sc A, 1 row sc F, 1 row sc E, 1 row sc K, 1 row dc K and G alternating across row, 5 rows dc G.

YOKE:

Starting at neck edge ch 57 (58, 61).

Row 1, right side: Dc in 4th ch from hook, dc in ea of next 7 (7, 8) ch (left front section); in next ch, make 2 dc, ch 2, and 2 dc; dc in ea of next 8 ch (sleeve); in next ch make 2 dc, ch 2, and 2 dc; dc in ea of next 17 (18, 19) ch (back); in next ch make 2 dc, ch 2, and 2 dc; dc in ea of next 8 ch (other sleeve); in next ch make 2 dc ch 2 and 2 dc dc in ea of rem 9 (9, 10) ch (right front). There are 67 (68, 71) dc, counting ch at beg of row as 1 dc. Ch 3, turn.

Row 2: Skip first dc, * dc in ea dc to within next ch 2 sp, in ch 2 sp make 2 dc, ch 2 and 2 dc. Rep from * three times more; dc in ea rem dc, dc in top of turning chain, 16 dc inc. Ch 3, turn.

Row 3: Rep Row 2, 99 (100, 103) dc. Always count ch 3 as 1 dc. Ch 3, turn.

Row 4: Skip first dc * dc in ea dc to within next ch 2 sp. In ch 2 sp make dc, ch 2, and dc. Rep from * three more times; dc in ea rem dc and in top of ch 3. 8 dc inc.

Rep last row (Row 4) eight (nine, ten) more times following color chart. 163 (180, 191) dc. There are 23 (25, 27) dc on ea front section; 36 (40, 42) dc on ea sleeve and 45 (50, 53) dc on back. Att B, ch 3, turn.

BODY:

Row 1: 1 Dc in first dc, dc in ea dc to within next ch 2 sp. 2 (2, 3) dc in sp. Skip sleeve sts, make 2 (2, 3) dc in next sp, dc in ea dc across back, 2 (2, 3) dc in next sp. Skip sleeve sts, 2 (2, 3) dc in next sp. Dc in ea rem dc; dc in top of ch 3. Att A, Ch 1, turn.

Row 2: Sc in ea sc around. Ch 1, turn.

Row 3: Work row of sc. Att F. Ch 1, turn.

Row 4: Work row of sc. Att E. Ch 1, turn.

Row 5: Work row sc. Att K. Ch 1, turn.

Row 6, increase round: Working in sc inc 1 sc in center of ea front and 3 sc inc across back evenly spaced. (To inc work 2 sc in sc of previous row.) Ch 3, turn.

Row 7: Skip first sc, 1 dc in next sc, dc in next but hold back last lp, att G and pull through to complete st (color change made). *Do not drop K* but carry along ea color not in use across back working over it. Continue alternating 2 G dc and 2K dc across row. Drop K and with G ch 3, turn, and dc for 5 rows. Ch 1, turn and work corded edge around bottom of jacket (See note at end.) End off.

SLEEVES:

Row 1: Att D at center of underarm from wrong side. Ch 3 and dc around. Att B. Sl st into 3rd ch of turning ch. Now working in rounds, ch 1, turn.

Row 2: Sc in ea dc. Att F. Join. Ch 3, turn.

Rows 3 and 4: Dc around. Att K. Join. Ch 3, turn.

Rows 5, 6, and 7: Dc around. Att J. Join. Ch 1, turn.

Rows 8, 9, and 10: Sc around. Att 2 strands Lavender worsted. Join. Ch 1, turn.

Row 11: 1 Sc in first sc * 1 sc in base of sc in row below, 1 sc in next sc; Rep from * arnd. Join. Ch 1, turn.

Row 12: Sc around. Att K. Join. Ch 3, turn.

Row 13: Dc around. Att I. Join. Ch 3, turn.

Row 14: Dc around. Att F. Join. Ch 3, turn.

Row 15: Dc around. Att J. Join. Ch 3, turn.

Rows 16, 17, and 18: Dc around. Att E. Join. Ch 3, turn.

Row 19: Dc around. Att J. Join. Ch 3, turn.

Rows 20 through 26: Worked in dc. Join. Ch 1, turn and work 1 row Sc. End off.

SKIRT:

Top Section. Measure waist, add 2″ and work chain of an uneven number. (*Do not twist chain.*) Join with sl st. Ch 1 and sc in 2nd ch from hook and in ea ch arnd. Join with sl st to ch 1. Ch 1, turn, and sc for 4 rows. Then inc every 5 sts evenly on 6th row. Join ch 3. Dc in ea sc arnd, join, ch 3, turn. Work 2nd row of dc arnd. Join, ch 1, turn. Now inc evenly spaced every 8th st. Join, ch 1, work now of sc (From here work even on these sts.) Join. Ch 3, turn and work as follows:

Middle Section: 2 rows dc, 2 rows sc, six more times. This skirt is midi-length (26".) To shorten, simply skip one or more sets of pattern rows. (Lower section is 9" from middle section to hem.)

Lower Section: End last 2 sc rows in A. Att I. Join.

Row 1: Holding I, sc in first sc, sc at base of next sc in row below (long sc), * sc in next sc, 1 sc at base of next sc in row below. Rep from * around. Join. Ch 1, turn.

Row 2: Work row of sc. Att E, and rep Rows 1 and 2. Att F. Rep Rows 1 and 2. Att A. Rep Rows 1 and 2. Join. Ch 2, turn. Dc in first sc, dc in next but hold back last lp. Att H. Pull through to complete st (color change made). Do not drop A but carry along ea color not in use across back. Working over it, cont alternating 2 A dc and 2 H dc across row. At end of row drop A and cont with H. Ch 2, turn.

Work row of dc, then 2 rows sc, 2 rows dc, 2 rows, sc, 2 rows dc, and 2 rows sc, then work corded edge. Sl st in turning chain and end off.

FINISHING:

Jacket. Work 3 rows sc around neckline with A. Now work row of sc from right side down ea front with G.

Skirt. Cut ribbon to fit waist of skirt leaving 1" overlap. Sew ribbon to inside of waistband ⅛" from edge of waistband along top and bottom edge of ribbon for casing, leaving opening for elastic. Thread elastic through casing and sew ends securely. Close opening of casing. Block both pieces lightly. (Lay damp cloth over garment and let dry overnight.)

Note: Corded edge st. Work a row of sc from left to right instead of from right to left.

Alpaca Coat

Sizes:

Directions are for sizes Small and Medium.

Materials:

Alpaca 100 percent wool yarn, 4-ply, 100-gram skeins.

Black (A)	9 (10) skeins
Rust (B)	1 skein
Beige (C)	1 skein
Brown (D)	4 skeins
Gray (E)	2 skeins

Variegated loop yarn 95 percent wool, 5 percent nylon, 2-oz. skeins skeins.

Black, Brown, Gray (F)	6 skeins

Frog closure.

Hook:

Size H aluminum or size to obtain gauge.

Gauge:

7 dc = 2″, 8 rows = 3″.

FRONT AND BACK PANELS:

Note: The body of the coat is worked vertically.

Make four, two for front and two for back. With A, ch 123 to measure approx 36″.

Row 1: 1 Hdc in 2nd ch from hook and in ea ch to end (122 hdc).
Rows 2 through 6: Hdc in ea hdc across, drop A. Att B, ch 1, turn.
Row 7: Work sc in ea hdc across. (This is the wrong side of the piece.) Ch 1, turn.
Row 8: Rep Row 7. Drop B. Att A, ch 2, turn.

Rows 9 and 10: Work hdc across. Drop A. Att C, ch 1, turn.
Rows 12 and 13: Work hdc across. Drop D. Att E, ch 2, turn.
Row 14: Work hdc across. Drop E. Att A, ch 1, turn.
Row 15: Sc across row. Drop A. Att D, ch 2, turn.
Rows 16 and 18: Work hdc across row. Drop D. Att C, ch 1, turn.
Row 19: Sc across row. Drop C. Att E, ch 2, turn.
Rows 20 and 21: Hdc across. Drop E. Att A, ch 2, turn.
Row 22: Hdc across. Drop A. Att C, ch 1, turn.
Row 23: Sc across row. End off. This row is the center back or front.

SIDE PANELS:

Make two for front. Ch 123 with A and work 4 rows of hdc. End off.

Att F to wrong side of first A row of any one of first 4 panels. This will now be a back panel. Ch 1 and work row of sc to end. Att A. Ch 2, turn and work 4 rows of hdc. End off. Repeat the same thing on another panel. These two panels will now be the back panels of the coat. Take both panels and place the two C rows together (center back), wrong sides facing. Be sure to line up the rows exactly. Now with F join the two panels together using the zig-zag stitch as follows:

Insert hook in 1 sc of one side, sl st once, insert hook in 1 sc of other side, sl st once. Continue to end. The two back panels are now joined.

FRONT PANELS:

On the remaining two panels and the remaining side panels place markers for pockets in this way. Remember that the C sc rows are center front. Lay out the two panels on a flat surface. Now lay the two side panels beside the fronts, A rows facing. On ea front and side panel along A rows place a marker 8 " down from top (or 28th st), and another on the 47th st (these are markers for pocket openings). Now with wrong sides facing and with color F work row of zig-zag st to join front and side panels. When you reach pocket markers stop zig-zag st but continue, (on *front panel only*) the 19 sts in sc. When you reach second marker resume joining sides with zig-zag. Be sure you have 19 sts left free on both front and side panels. End off.

Work other side the same way.

YOKE:

Starting at neck edge with A, ch 63.

Row 1: Hdc in 3rd ch from hook and in ea of next 10 ch (left front) in next ch work 2 hdc, ch 1 and 2 hdc (double inc made) hdc in ea of next 8 ch (left sleeve); work double inc in next ch, hdc in ea of next 18 (back); work double inc in next ch, hdc in ea of next 8 ch (right sleeve); work double inc in next ch, hdc in ea of next 11 ch for front (72 hdc counting turning ch as 1 hdc). Ch 2, turn.

Row 2: * Hdc in ea hdc to next ch 1 sp; in ch 1 sp work hdc, ch 1, and hdc (single inc made). Rep from * three times more, hdc in ea hdc across hdc in turning ch (8 hdc inc). Ch 2, turn.

Row 3: * Hdc in ea hdc to next ch 1 sp. Work double inc in ch 1 sp. Rep from * three times more. Hdc in ea hdc across and in turning ch. Ch 2, turn, rep 2nd and 3rd rows nine times more ending on double inc row. End off. Place markers in ch 1 spaces to indicate start of sleeves.

SLEEVES:

Att yarn A to ch 1 sp at sleeve marker on right side of yoke.

Row 1: Ch 2, 2 hdc in next hdc and then 1 hdc in ea hdc, 2 hdc in last st and 1 hdc under ch 1 sp. Ch 2, turn.

Row 2: Work 1 row hdc including 1 in turning ch. Ch 2, turn.

Row 3: Work another row hdc. Att B. Ch 1, turn.

Rows 4 and 5: Work sc across. Att F. Ch 1, turn.

Rows 6 and 7: Work sc across. Att A. Ch 2, turn.

Rows 8 and 9: Hdc across. Att C. Ch 1, turn.

Row 10: Sc across. Att D. Ch 2, turn.

Rows 11 through 14: Hdc across. Att A. Ch 2, turn.

Row 15: Hdc across. Att F. Ch 1, turn.

Rows 16 through 18: Sc across. Att E. Ch 2, turn.

Rows 19 through 22: Hdc across. Att C. Ch 1, turn.

Row 23: Sc across. Att D. Ch 2, turn.

Rows 24 through 26: Hdc across. Att A. Ch 1, turn.

Row 27: Sc across row. Att E. Ch 2, turn.

Row 28: Hdc across. Att D. Ch 2, turn.

Rows 29 through 30: Hdc across. Att F. Ch 1, turn.

Rows 31 through 34: Sc across. Att A. Ch 2, turn.

Rows 35 through 36: Hdc across. Att B. Ch 1, turn.

Row 37: Sc across. Att D. Ch 2, turn.

Rows 38 and 39: Hdc across. Att A. Ch 2, turn.

Rows 40 through 46: Hdc across. Att F. Ch 1, turn.

Work in sc for 6 rows or to desired length. End off.

Work other sleeve the same.

COLLAR:

Ch 33 with F. Hdc until piece measures 18" or length to fit neckline. End off.

Finishing: Work row of sc along top of back panel and two front panels, working sc into the ends of hdc rows (picking up a thread from second hdc and working over first) and between sc rows. Be careful not to stretch panels; keep tension even. Place marker at center back of yoke. Line up to center back of panel, using the first B rows of sleeves as your guide. Join with zig-zag stitch. Each front panel should line up with center front edge of yoke and first B row of sleeve.
Line up and pin, then join side seams from right side. Sew sleeve seams from wrong side.

POCKETS:

From the wrong side join A to top of pocket opening on the skipped sts of A row, ch 1, sc to end of opening and into the next 5 sts of seams (picking up 1 thread of st), ch 2, turn, and working on these 24 sts, hdc for 11 rows. End off.

FINISHING:

Work row of sc around neckline, dec over ch 1 sp (draw up a lp in st before ch 1 space, and draw up another lp after ch 1 sp, dec made). Att collar to neckline from right side.
With F, work row of sc from right side along center front opening including collar. Ch 1, turn, and work a 2nd row. Then one more row of sc, ch 2, turn, work 1 row hdc. Join yarn to last row where neckline and collar meet and hdc down front for 2 rows, then 1 row sc. End off. Rep on other side.

Sew on frog closing at center front where yoke and front panels meet.

Pot Pourri Jacket

Sizes:

Directions are for Small. Directions for Medium and Large are in parentheses.

Measurements:

18″ across back at underarm. The back is double the width of the two unfinished fronts. Pattern is worked from the top down.

Materials:

4-ply Sport-weight yarn, 2-oz. skeins.

Coral (A)	1 skein
Cherry (B)	1 skein
Cranberry (C)	1 skein
Orange (D)	1 skein

Cotton and viscose chenille, 1-oz. balls.

Gold (E)	1 ball
Wine (F)	1 ball

#3 Line braid (rayon ribbon) spool.

Dark Wine (G)	½ spool
Terra-cotta (H)	½ spool

Brushed wool variegated yarn, 2-oz. skeins.

Scarlet (I)	2 skeins

Hook:

Size H aluminum or size to obtain gauge.

Gauge:

4 patterns = 2″.

Note: Read all instructions before starting. A word about blocking: The Pot Pourri Jacket is tricky to do because of the mix of yarns used. In this case just use a whiff of steam from your iron for the edges and pin down overnight. Blocking the brushed wool garments is not recommended because they tend to stretch if they have gotten too damp. It is good to remember these precautions when having garments drycleaned or when washing them by hand at home.

BACK:

With A ch 64, 1 dc in 4th ch from hook * 1 sc in ea of next 2 ch, 1 dc in ea of next 2 ch, rep from * to end. Ch 1, turn.

Row 2: 1 Sc in ea of first 2 dc, * 1 dc in ea of next 2 sc, 1 sc in ea of next 2 dc. Rep from * ending 1 sc in last dc, 1 sc in top of turning ch. Ch 2, turn.

Row 3: Skip first sc, 1 dc in next sc, * 1 sc in ea of next 2 dc, 1 dc, in ea of next 2 sc, rep from * to end. Ch 1, turn (Pattern st completed).

Rep Rows 2 and 3 for pattern, changing colors as follows: 3 rows A, 7 rows B, and 12 rows C. Att. H and work 2 rows, 2 rows D, 1 row E. Ch 1, turn. Work 1 row sc I, ch 2, turn, work 1 row dc. Ch 1, turn. Work 1 row sc. Ch 1, turn. Att G and work in Pattern st, ch 1, turn.

Now work 3 rows B in Pattern st. Att H and work 2 rows in Pattern st. Att I. Ch 2, turn. Work 1 row of dc. Att F, work 1 row of Pattern st. Att G and work 2 rows Pattern st.

SHOULDER:

Att A to starting ch at top of jacket. Ch 2 and work Pattern st for 4½″. Work other shoulder.

FRONTS:

Ch 32 for each front and work as for back. Work shoulder on each front as for back. Sl st shoulder seams together from wrong side in back loop of ea stitch.

SLEEVES:

Att C bet last A row and first H row. Ch 1. Work row of sc from right side of garment (63 sc). Ch 2, turn. Work in pattern for 6 rows. Now work 1 row H in pattern; 1 sc row in D; 1 row

popcorns. (See Note at end of instructions.) Sc 1 row, 1 row dc E, 1 row sc I; 1 row dc I; 1 row sc I; 1 row Pattern st G; 1 row sc B; 1 row popcorns; 1 row sc, all in B, 2 rows in pattern H; 2 rows dc with I; 1 row F; 2 rows in pattern with G; next cont with G and work 1 row sc; 1 row Corded Edge st. (See Note at end of instructions.)

Finishing: Work row of sc around neck from right side with A. Att B. Ch 1, turn. Work row of sc dec 1 st before shoulder seam and 1 st after. Cont around dec 1 st at center back and 1 st before next shoulder seam and 1 st after. Cont to end. Ch 1, turn. Work 1 row even. Ch 1, turn. Work 1 row popcorns. Att H. Ch 1, turn. Work row of sc. Do not turn and work row of corded edge.

FRONTS:

Att B to edge of neckline at bottom of collar (from right side) and work row of sc down front of jacket. Ch 1, turn. Work 2 sc then cont in Popcorn st to top of front. Ch 1, turn. Work row of sc. Att H and ch 1, turn. Work row of sc, then without turning at end of row work back in corded edge. End off. Work other front the same. Sew side and sleeve seams very carefully with matching thread.

Note:

Row 1, *Popcorn stitch:* 1 Sc in first sc * in next sc (yo, draw up loop, yo and through 2 loops) five times, yo and through 6 loops. Ch 1, sc in ea of next 2 sc. Rep from *, ending 1 sc in ea of last 2 sc, ch 1, turn.

Row 2: 1 Sc in ea sc and in ea ch 1, ending 1 sc in last sc.

Corded Edge: Work a row of sc from left to right instead of from right to left end sl st in last st.

Linda Osborne Blood

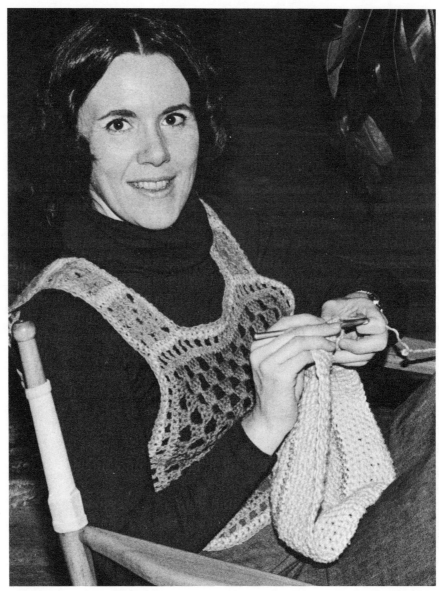

Linda Osborne Blood majored in fashion design at the Massachusetts College of Art, receiving her BFA in 1966. After moving to New York City later the same year, she worked at a variety of creative jobs in such diverse places as a pattern company, a rural New England hand-weaving studio, and a major textile firm before striking out in her chosen field. In addition to her career as a top-ranking crochet designer, Linda is an expert weaver and a macramé artist.

If you haven't run across Linda Blood's designs, you're not reading women's magazines. Those that have carried her designs include Ladies' Home Journal Needle & Craft, Ladies' Home Journal, Woman's Day, Family Circle, Good Housekeeping Needlecraft, McCall's Needlework and Crafts, and Glamour.

"*I* go through periods where I'll sit down and simply pour out a whole bunch of ideas on paper. Later on I'll go through all those sketches and notes and throw out the ones that just don't make it and keep the ones that do. These periods of designing usually coincide with the upcoming fashion seasons. I look through all the current fashion magazines, both from here and Europe. I really enjoy keeping up with all the newest trends. I think of it as a kind of game; that way I keep from being overly serious about that aspect of my work.

"When I work for the magazines, I sketch and 'swatch' a lot of things. Then I send them off to the editors I work with and wait for the reactions. Or sometimes an editor or a fashion director for a yarn company will call me up. They'll have some feelings about the sort of thing they want for a future issue or brochure, and I'll take their germ of an idea, sit down with it, develop it, and execute a design in the yarn they want me to work with. More often than not I come up with the kind of thing they're looking for, and the kind of thing their readers and customers are looking for.

"I always keep in mind that most of the people who follow my designs don't crochet nearly full-time as I do. So I try to gear my things to the way the average crocheter works. As long as I can do this without making the crochet look average, I think I'm doing my job."

Linda Osborne Blood

Rainbow Stripe Coat
with Matching Hat

Size:

Directions are for Medium size. Small and Large sizes are in parentheses.

Measurement around body from center point as worn, closed, is 40″ (37½″, 44″).

Underarm to hem: 34″ (33″, 35″ or as preferred).

Sleeve width: 17″ (15″, 18″).

Sleeve length, underarm to top of fringe: 15″ (14¼″, 15¾″).

Hat: One size fits all.

See Ground Rules below for further information.

Materials:

Total of about 5½ lbs. (88 oz.) bulky-weight yarns or yarns that can be combined to equate them. About 25 oz. of this in one color for edgings and hat, the rest (about 4 lbs.) in various colors, depending on personal preference.

Hook:

Size K aluminum or size to obtain gauge.

Gauge:

11 post dcs = 4″ (blocked), 6 rows = 3″.

11 scs = 4″, 10 rows = 3″.

Use main color yarn to set gauge.

This coat was designed for two main purposes:
• as an excuse to buy all that great yarn you've never been able to justify buying before, because how were you going to use it all up? Now you can buy small amounts of each type and use it all up in one project. (Or, as in my case, to use up the stuff that's been sitting around the house for years.)
• to crochet a garment entirely in stripes without having to weave in a million little row ends. The obvious solution: fringe.

Ground Rules:

1. When choosing yarn, start with the main color yarn that will go for the edgings and hat, and match the other colors to it. Any arrangement of colors can be used: a rainbow stripe such as the one shown, variations on a single color, or an all-natural color "handspun" look. A good-quality wool is the best fiber, but cotton, linen, silk, novelties, and synthetics will add interest to the stripes.

2. Fringe: Each row is begun and ended with a "tail" of yarn about 8″ to 9″ long. As each row is finished, cut two more strands of double that length, draw one through each end and knot up close to the stitches.

3. Turn all rows. Starting them all on the same side results in a marked list to starboard.

4. Basically, this coat is a "T-cut"—straight through the body with sleeves added at right angles—because increases and decreases for body shaping would break up the flow of the stripes. But if you want to get really subtle about it, go down one hook size for the area from just below the waist to about halfway up the sleeve. This will narrow it from the hips through the bust. Return to the original hook for the upper sleeve section to give the top of the sleeve a slight downward curve.

The striped section is done first, then the edgings.

With Main color (MC), leaving "tail," chain 106 (100, 116), cut, leaving "tail," pull last chain tight. 105 (99, 115) chains left. Turn. Change colors as desired, leaving fringe at each end, turning all rows:

Row 1: Dc in each chain.

Row 2: Sc in 1st dc, dc around posts of next 103 (97, 113) dcs at front of work (toward you), sc in last dc.

Row 3: Sc in 1st sc, dc around posts of all dcs at back of work (away from you), sc in last sc.

Rows 4 through 58 (56, 60) or desired length (5″ edging will be added): Rep Rows 2 and 3. There will be a smooth vertical look to one side and a strong horizontal ridge on the other. Use whichever you prefer as the "right" side. (The sample garment uses the vertical.)

FRONT SLEEVES:

Mark 25th (24th, 27th) st in from each side.

Row 59 (57, 61): Sc in 1st sc, work in patt to marked st, sc in marked st, ch 40 (38, 42), cut and pull last ch tight. Total 39 (37, 41) chs.

Row 60 (58,62): Dc in ea ch to 1st sc, dc in sc, work in patt across rest of row.

Rows 61 through 77 (59 through 73, 63 through 81): Work even in patt. Try to end with a row of MC.

Work other side to match, reversing shaping.

BACK—SHOULDERS AND SLEEVES:

Row 59 (57, 61): Ch 39 (37, 41), sc in marked st, work in patt across back, sc in other marked st, ch 40, (38, 42), cut, pull tight.

Work rest of back to correspond to front sleeves. Sl st top and underarm sleeve seams (suggest on right side for top, wrong side for underarm). Trim fringe evenly. Block, or just press.

EDGINGS:

Front: With MC, right side facing, start at lower edge.

Row 1: Working around the sides of the sc to that the fringe will be pushed to the front, sc in side of each row up to the last row before the shoulder seam, ch 1, turn.

Row 2: Dec 1 sc over next 2 sts (draw up a loop in each, draw through all loops on hook), sc to end of row, ch 1, turn.

Row 3: Sc in each sc to last 2, dec 1 sc over last 2, ch 1, turn.

Rows 4 through 7: Rep Rows 2 and 3.

Rows 8 through 13: Work even in sc. Break off. Weave in loose ends. Work other side to match, reversing neck shaping. Press edgings.

Hem: With MC, sc evenly across hem. Work even in sc for 16 more rows (or to desired length). Break off.

Ties: Make six. Ch about 18″ with MC, cut, press, attach three to each side where desired, knot ends.

Collar ties: Change colors and leave fringe as before. Ch 84. With right side facing, work 5 dc over sides of Rows 1–7 (dec rows) of edging at neck, dc in ea st across back neck, 5 dc over dec rows of other edging, ch 85, pull tight, cut. Work about 7″ in patt as body of coat. Sl st over last row.

HAT:

Start at top. With MC and K hook, ch 4, join with sl st to 1st ch to form ring. Now work in spiral.

Round 1: Work 2 scs in each ch (8 scs).

Round 2: Work 2 scs in each sc (16 scs).

Round 3: Sc in each sc.

Round 4: * Sc in next sc, 2 scs in next sc, rep from * around (24 scs).

Round 5: Rep Round 3.

Round 6: * Sc in next 2 scs, 2 scs in next sc (32 scs).

Round 7: Rep Round 3.

Round 8: * Sc in next 3 scs, 2 scs in next sc (40 scs).

Round 9: Rep Round 3.

Round 10: * Sc in next 4 scs, 2 scs in next sc (48 scs).

Round 11: Rep Round 3.

Round 12: * Sc in next 5 scs, 2 scs in next sc (56).

Rounds 13 through 15: Rep Round 3. At end of Round 15, ch 1.

Round 16: Dc in each sc, sl st in ch 1.

Round 17: Dc around post of each dc at front, s1 st in ch 1, ch 1.

Rounds 18 through 20: Rep Round 17.

Sl st in each dc, and in ch 1 break off, weave in loose ends. Wear hat with preferred side out.

Block on hat block or wig form if available.

Afghan Stitch Vest

Size:

Directions are for Medium size (bust 36″ measured blocked and closed). Changes for Small (bust 32″) and Large (bust 40″) sizes are in parentheses.

Materials:

Heavyweight mohair, knitting worsted, or any other soft yarn that will give gauge.

Main color (White): about ½ lb. (8 oz.)

Stripe colors: about 1 oz. each of Green, Red, Orange, Gold, and Tweed novelty.

Hook:

Size K aluminum, 10″ or 14″ (may also be designated as 10½ or 7.00mm) afghan hook or size to obtain gauge.

Gauge:

3 stitches = 1″.
(Make a swatch to test both the gauge and the "knit" pattern stitch by chaining about 18 and working as for Rows 1 through 17.)

Note: This garment is made entirely of straight pieces which are then joined at shoulders and sides. Adjustments for length and armhole depth can be made before seams are closed. Collar is added last.

The surface will have the appearance of a knit, and a strong horizontal ridge will appear on the underside. The vest will not stretch, however, as a knit will. Instead the even distribution of weight and "thermal" effect of the ridges will produce a very stable, light, and warm garment.

The vest is started at the hem and worked up to the shoulders.

With White, ch 55 (50, 62). (If chaining with the long hook feels awkward, use a regular K hook and slip the last ch off into the afghan hook.)

Row 1: Insert the hook under one strand of the 2nd ch from the hook *from back to front*, yo and draw through a loop from the front to the back. (If the first row is started this way, instead of inserting the hook from front to back as is usual, the garment will *not* curl up from the bottom once it is blocked. Otherwise, it *will*. Consequently, it is *very* important to insert the hook *from back to front*!) Repeat this process in each of the remaining loops.

To work off loops: Yo, draw through 1 loop, * yo, draw through 2 loops, rep from * all across row until there is only 1 loop left on hook. This will count as the first loop of the next row.

Row 2: Skip the 1st vertical loop (at the far right) of the previous row and * insert hook from front to back between the 2 upright bars of the next vertical loop, yo, draw up a loop from the back to the front. Rep from * across row, end by inserting the hook through the last st at the left and drawing up a loop. Work off loops same as for Row 1.

(Some instruction books direct you to ch 1 at the start of a row. I can't think why, as this produces a very pronounced and totally useless curve at the right side of the piece. Don't.)

Rows 1 through 17: Rep Row 2 for Knit Pattern Stitch (KPS). As you may recall, I stated that a properly started afghan stitch piece will not curl up *once it is blocked*. Before is another matter—right now it probably resembles a scroll. If this is difficult to work with, slip the hook off at the end of a row, pin the piece to a towel, lay a damp cloth over it and steam it lightly. *Do not touch the last completed row with the iron.* It will make a mark when you start up again. When the piece is dry, resume work.

At end of Row 17, change colors. Work off all but the last 2 loops of the row, cut first color, draw through the last loop with the second color, tie ends to secure, and continue. Use this method whenever changing colors.

Row 18: KPS, Orange.

Row 19: KPS, Red.

Row 20: KPS, Gold. Do not change color at end.

RIDGE STITCH:

Row 21: Gold. This is actually a backwards "knit" row. Insert the hook through the same loops as for the KPS, but from back to front, drawing through the loops from front to back. A horizontal ridge will form (RS). Work off loops as usual.

Row 22: KPS, Green.

Row 23: KPS, Tweed novelty.

Row 24: KPS, Orange.

Row 25: KPS, Gold.

Row 26: KPS, Red.

Row 27: KPS, Tweed novelty.

Row 28: RS, Green.

Row 29: KPS, Gold.

Row 30: LPS, Orange.

Row 31: KPS, Red.

Row 32: KPS, Tweed novelty.

Row 33: KPS, Green.

Row 34: KPS, Orange.

Row 35: RS, Orange.

Row 36: KPS, Red.

Row 37: KPS, Gold.

Rows 38 through 64 (60, 68): KPS, White. Check for length here—add or rip a few rows if necessary. To finish shoulders, sl st over first 17 (15, 19) st, break off and secure, sl st over last 17 (15, 19) st, break off and secure.

FRONT PIECES:

Make two. Chain 29 (27, 33) with White and work to match back. Sl st over opposite sides to match back shoulders.

Block all pieces; don't steam them them too hard or you will squash the ridges.

Join shoulder seams, either by weaving the slip stitches together on the right side, which produces a decorative raised seam, or by slip stitching them together on the wrong side, which produces an invisible one. Side seams should be woven together on right side, carefully matching rows, from hem to top of stripes.

COLLAR:

Attach White to hook and pick up sts around neck edge as if it were Row 1. There should be about 43 to 45 (40 to 43, 45 to 47) sts, depending on what you pick up at the seams. Work off loops. Work about 8 more rows, then sl st over last row and break off. Weave in any loose ends.

TIES:

Using colors to match ridge rows, ch about 12″ for each of six ties, press, let dry, knot one end. (Once steam pressed, the ties should stretch out to about 13″ to 14″.) Attach loose ends to matching ridge rows.

If one front side of the vest is a little longer than the other, pin the short side out to the proper length, press, and allow to dry.

Basketweave Hooded Jacket

Size:

Directions are for Medium size. Changes for Small and Large are in parentheses.
Bust: 36" (32", 40").
Underarm to hem: 19" (18", 20").
Sleeve width: 14½" (12", 16").
Sleeve length: 19" (18", 20").
Armhole depth: 8" (6½", 8½").

Materials:

Homespun Donegal wool tweed or any comparable weight yarn. About 2¼ lbs. (36 oz.) total for size Medium (about ¼ lb. less for Small, ¼ lb. more for Large).

Main Color (A)	1¾ lbs. (about 28 oz.)
Gold (B)	about ¼ lb. (4 oz.)
Rust (C)	about ¼ lb. (4 oz.)
Gold Mix (D)	about ¼ lb. (4 oz.)
Blue Mix (E)	about ¼ lb. (4 oz.)

The size of this garment is determined by hook size and gauge.

Hooks:

For size Medium, H and J.
For size Small, G and I.
For size Large, I and K.

Gauge:

Size Medium:
   H hook: 7 scs = 2", 10 rows sc = 2".
          7 dcs = 2", 6 rows dc = 3".
   J hook: 15 post dcs = 5", 6 post dc
          rows = 3½".
Size Small:
   G hook: 4 scs = 1", 4 rows sc = ¾".
          4 dcs = 1", 6 rows dc = 3".

I hook: 7 post dcs = 2", 8 post dc
    rows = 3¼".
Size Large:
    I hook: 10 scs = 3", 6 rows sc =
        1½".
        10 dcs = 3", 6 rows dc =
        3¾".
    K hook: 8 post dcs = 3", 8 post dc
        rows = 3¾".

BACK:

Start at top and work down. With A and larger hook ch 58.

Row 1: Dc in 3rd ch from hook and in each remaining ch (57 dcs counting ch 2 as 1 dc). Ch 1, turn.

Row 2: Skip 1st st, * dc around post of next dc at front (toward you), dc around post of next at back (away from you), rep from * across ending with a front dc, sc in top of ch, ch 1, turn.

Row 3: Skip 1st st, * dc around post of next st back, dc around post of next st front, rep from * across, ending with a back dc, sc in ch, ch 1, turn.

Rows 4 through 19: Rep Rows 2 and 3. (This is the "dc post rib" pattern.)

BASKETWEAVE:

Row 20: Skip 1st st, * dc around posts of next 5 dcs at back, dc around posts of next 5 at front, rep from * across, ending with 5 back dcs, sc in ch, ch 1, turn.

Row 21: Skip 1st st, * dc around posts of next 5 at front, dc around posts of next 5 at back, rep from * across, ending with 5 front dcs, sc in ch, ch 1, turn.

Row 22: Rep Row 20.

Row 23: Rep Row 21.

Row 24: Rep Row 21. (This changes each 5–st block from "front" to "back" or vice-versa.)

Row 25: Rep Row 20.

Row 26: Rep Row 21.

Row 27: Rep Row 20.

Rows 28 through 55: Rep from Row 20. (A pattern or alternate 5–st, 4-row blocks will form.)

Row 56: Skip 1st st, dc in each dc and in ch, ch 1, turn.

Rows 57 through 61: Rep Rows 2 and 3. Break off.

FRONT:

Make two. Ch 18, work same as back (except begin basket-weave with 5 *front* dcs) on 17 sts.

SLEEVES:

Make two. With larger hook, ch 43.

Row 1: Dc in 3rd ch from hook and each remaining ch (42 dcs).
Rows 2 through 29: Starting Row 2 with 5 front dcs, work in basketweave patt on 42 sts. Break off at end of Row 29, turn.

PATTERN BAND:

Row 30: With E and smaller hook, sc in each st of Row 29, ch 1, turn.
Row 31: Sc in 1st 7 scs, sl st in next sc, ch 1, turn.
To change colors, draw through last loop of st before color change with new color. Carry inactive colors at back, working over them at least every other st.
Row 32: Skip sl st, sl st in next sc, sc in next 2 scs, sc in next with A, sc in next 3 with D, ch 1, turn.
Row 33: First 2 scs with D, next 1 with A, next 2 with E, sl st in next sc, ch 1, turn.
Row 34: Skip sl st, sl st in next sc, sc in next 2 scs, next sc with A, last sc with D, drop D, pick up A, ch 1, turn.
Row 35: Sc with A in 1st sc, next 2 scs in E, sl st in next sc, ch 1, turn.
Row 36: All E, skip sl st, sl st in next sc, sc in last 2 scs, ch 1, turn.
Row 37: Sc in 1st sc, sl st in next, ch 1, turn.
Row 38: Skip sl st, sc in next sc, ch 1, turn.
Row 39: Sl st in sc, break off. Cut any other colors still attached.
Work a piece on the other (right) side of the sleeve to match this one, reversing the shaping.

CENTER TRIANGLE:

Start with E. Work Row 30 of Pattern Band.
Row 31: Sl st in the 7th free sc of Row 30, sc in next 12 scs, sl st in next sc (which will be the 7th free sc in from the other side), ch 1, turn.
Row 32: Skip sl st, sl st in next sc, sc in next 2 scs, next sc with A, next 4 scs with D, next sc with A, next 2 scs with E, sl st in next sc, ch 1, turn.

Row 33: Skip sl st, sl st in next sc, sc in next 2 scs, sc in next sc with A, next 2 scs with D, next sc with A, next 2 scs with E, sl st in next, ch 1, turn.

Row 34: Skip sl st, sl st in next sc, sc in next 2 scs, next sc with A, next 3 scs with E, sl st in next, ch 1, turn.

Row 35: All E, skip sl st, sl st in next sc, sc in next 4 scs, sl st in next sc, ch 1, turn.

Row 36: Skip sl st, sl st in next sc, sc in next 2 scs, sl st in next sc, ch 1, turn.

Row 37: Skip sl st, sl st in next sc, ch 1, turn.

Row 38: Sl st in sc, break off. Press this last section lightly. The curves now formed are for the "rainbows" to fit into. You will need 11 "rainbows," so it is a good idea to make them all now.

RAINBOWS:

With smaller hook and B ch 3.

Row 1: Work 5 dcs in 1st ch (makes 6 dcs including 2 chs at end), break off, turn.

Row 2: With D, sl st and ch 2 in 1st dc, dc in same dc, 2 dcs in rem dcs and in top of ch 2, break off, turn.

Row 3: With C, sl st and ch 2 in 1st dc, dc in same dc, * dc in next dc, 2 dcs in next st, rep from * around row, break off, turn.

Row 4: With E, sl st and ch 2 in 1st dc, dc in each dc and in top of ch 2, break off, turn.

Row 5: With A, sl st and ch 2 in 1st dc, dc in next st, * 2 dcs in next st, dc in next st, rep from * around, break off, turn.

Row 6: With B, sl st and ch 2 in 1st dc, dc in each dc, break off.

Attaching "rainbows" to sleeves: With right sides of both pieces facing, with C and smaller hook, sc in the first 6 dcs on the right side of a "rainbow," sc the rest of the rainbow as evenly as possible to one of the curves at the edge of the sleeve, by working through both together, around to the 6th dc of the "rainbow" on the other side, sc in the last 6 dcs, ch 1, turn. Pick up another "rainbow," sc through both together for first 6 sts, sc to other curve, sc in last 6 dcs, break off. Work other sleeve in same manner.

CUFF:

With A and larger hook, work 43 dcs as evenly as possible across the lower edge of the "rainbows." Work next 5 rows in the "dc post rib" pattern. Break off.

FRONT PATTERN BANDS:

These are basically the same as the ones on the sleeve, except that they are worked into the sides of rows and each has 1 more "rainbow" than each sleeve.

Right-hand side as worn: With E and smaller hook, work as evenly as possible 70 scs, right side facing, into the sides of the rows from the lower edge to about 2"–2½", down from the top, sl st in side of next row, ch 1, turn.

Rows 2 through 9: Rep Rows 32 through 39 of *center* part of sleve patt band. Then, with E, skip next 6 scs on base row, sl st in next, sc in next 12, sl st in next, ch 1, turn.

Rows 3 through 9: Rep 33 through 39 of center section on sleeve panel. Skip another 6 scs, rep once more. Skip another 6 scs, and work a half-section like the second one you did on the sleeve. This should just finish off the row.

Attach the "rainbows" to the curves the same as for the sleeves.

These sections will be rather puckery, both on the sleeves and the front pieces. Block each piece carefully, pinning it out so that all the sides are even. Blocking on the ribbing and basketweave sections should be done lightly so as not to flatten the stitches, but with these pattern bands you just can't beat laying a damp cloth over them and steam-pressing the living daylights out of them. Allow to dry thoroughly before resuming work.

HOOD:

This is a *big* hood, almost a half-circle. (If you are making a size Large and don't want too huge a hood, I recommend using the H rather than the I hook for it.)

Pick up that 11th "rainbow."

Row 7: With C, smaller hook, right side facing, sc *over* each dc so it looks the way it does when you attach it to the curves. Break off.

You will notice that Row 5 of the rainbow features an increase (2 dcs in 1) every other st. For the following Rows 8 through 19, starting and ending the rows the same way you did on the rainbow, work:

Row 8: D, inc every 3rd st.

Row 9: Even, in C.

Row 10: E, inc every 4th st.

Row 11: Even, in A.

Row 12: B, inc every 5th st.

Row 13: C, rep Row 7.
Row 14: Even, in D.
Row 15: C, inc every 6th st.
Row 16: Even, in E.
Row 17: A, inc every 7th st.
Row 18: Even, in D.
Row 19: C, rep Row 7.
Rows 20 through 35: E, even in sc. Break off.

Work 15 scs along the sides of the E rows in E, change to A, sc in each of the dc rows (1 sc in side of each row to gather this section in so it will fit into the neck). Change back to E, 15 scs along other sides of sc rows. Press hood lightly.

FINISHING:

Across top of back, right side facing, with A and larger hook, work around posts of Row 1 dcs at front of work: sc in first 5, hdc in next 5, dc in next 47, hdc in next 5, sc in last 5. Break off. Work over front top edges to match. This is to slant the shoulders. Sl st, or sc, shoulder seams together on wrong side and press. In same manner, sl st tops of sleeves to corresponding armhole "dc post rib" sections and press. Sl st underarm and side seams, carefully matching squares, to top of third square up on body, or close it all the way if you prefer. Press, and weave in any loose ends. Work 15 scs in E along 1 side of neck curve, same number of scs in A around back neck as there are in A on edge of hood, 15 more E along other neck curve. Using same color yarns, sl st or sc hood to neck matching these color sections, and press.

Front ribbing: With larger hook, A, right side facing, work about 67 dcs spaced evenly to neck seam, 85 around hood, 67 down other side. (Total must be an uneven number.) Work 4 more rows in the "dc post rib" pattern, sl st around last row. Ribbing should curve in a little; it will straighten out when pressed.

Ties: With A, ch six ties, each about 18", and press. Attach at desired points on front. Knot ends.

Fancy-Collar Pullover

Size:

Directions are for Medium size. Changes for Small and Large sizes are in parentheses.

Bust: 35″ (31″, 39″)—loose-fitting.
Sleeve width: 13″ (11¾″, 14¼″).
Sleeve length: (with cuff) 18″ (17″, 19″).
Underarm to hem: 14″ (13″, 15″).
Shoulder (dropped): 6″ (5½″, 6½″).

Materials:

2-ply Sport-weight yarn or equivalent.
Main color—Beige (A) 11 to 12 oz. (Small, 10 to 11; Large, 12 to 13.)
Small amounts—about 1 to 2 oz. each of seven other colors:

Dark Brown (A)
Light Taupe (B)
Pumpkin (C)
Champagne (D)
Dark Green (E)
Light Brick (F)
Rust (G)

Hooks:

Sizes G and H aluminum or sizes to obtain gauge.

Gauge:

H hook, 11 dcs = 3″, 2 rows = 1″.

Note: Garment can be made either as a plain turtleneck pullover or with the fancy collar, which is added last. Notations of slight changes for the plain version are included in the text. Start at lower edge.

BACK:

With G hook and A, ch 64 (58, 72).

Row 1: Dc in 3rd ch from hook and in rem ch, 63 (57, 71) st, counting ch 2. Ch 1, turn.

Row 2: Skip 1st dc, dc around the post of the next dc at front (toward you), * dc around the post of the next dc at back (away from you), dc around next at front, rep from * across row, end with sc in top of ch, ch 1, turn.

Row 3: Skip 1st st, dc around next at back, * dc around next at front, dc around next at back, rep from * across row, sc in ch, ch 1, turn.

Row 4: Skip 1st st, dc around next at front, * dc around next at back, dc around next at front, sc in ch, ch 1, turn.

Rows 5 through 7: Rep Rows 3, 4, 3. (If working plain turtleneck, add 2 more rows in this stitch.) Change to H hook. At end of Row 7, ch 2, turn.

Row 8: Dc in 1st st, dc in ea dc and twice in ch at end. Turn.

Row 9: Sl st and ch 2 in 1st dc, dc in ea rem dc and in ch, turn.

Rows 10 through 48 (46, 50): Rep Row 9 (work even in dc).

Row 49 (47, 51): 7(6, 8) scs, 7 (6, 8) hdcs, 37 (35, 41) dcs, 7 (6, 8) hdcs, 7 (6, 8) scs. Break off.

FRONT:

Work same as back through Row 43 (41, 43).

NECK SHAPING:

Mark center stitch for reference.

Row 44 (42, 44): Dc in 1st 24 (21, 27) sts, dec 1 dc over next 2 sts: * yarn over (yo), insert hook in next st, yo, draw up a loop, yo, draw through 2 loops on hook, rep from *, yo, draw through all loops on hook. Ch 2, turn.

Row 45 (43, 45): In same manner, dec 1 st over 1st 2 sts, dc to end of row, turn.

Row 45 (44, 46,): Dc across, end with dec of 1 st over last 2, ch 2, turn.

Row 47 (45, 47): Rep Row 45 (43, 45).

Row 48 (46, Rows 48 through 50): Work even in dc, turn.

Row 49 (47, 51): 8 (7, 10) dc, 7 (6, 8) hdc, 7 (6, 8) sc, break off.

Work other side to match, reversing shaping.

SLEEVES:

Make two. With G hook ch 32 (28, 36).

Rows 1 through 6: Same as back and front on 31 (27, 35) sts. (If plain version, add 2 more rows.)

Change to H hook. At end of Row 6, ch 2, turn.

Row 7: Dc in 1st 2 sts, 2 dc in next, * dc in next, 2 dcs in next, rep from * across. Should have 47 (43, 51) sts.

Rows 8 through 43 (41, 45): Work even in dc, break off.

Block all pieces lightly. Do not flatten ribbing.

SEAMS:

This garment has a prominent outside seam to balance the strong collar. If you prefer an invisible seam, slip-stitch the seam on the wrong, rather than the right, side. To start, sl st shoulder seams together and press. To prepare sides of pieces, work scs on a ratio of 3 in the side of every 2 rows (that is, 2 in 1 row, 1 in the next) of dc, 1 in the side of each post st dc row (rib). Start the sleeves by slip-stitching around the lower edge of the cuff. When scs are complete, sl st the seams together, not too tightly; use a larger hook if necessary. Press.

TURTLENECK:

Row 1: With H hook, work about 63 (63, 67) dcs, spaced as evenly as possible around neck edge. Ch 1, turn.

Rows 2 through 19: Work even in dc post rib same as for cuff and hem. (For plain style, add 2 more rows, sl st or sc over last row, break off. Weave in loose ends.)

FANCY COLLAR:

At end of Row 19, ch 3, turn.

Row 20: Work a tr (yo twice) into dc next to ch 3. Work 2 tr into each dc around, sl st in top of ch, break off. (If you think you might prefer a somewhat smaller and flatter collar than the one shown, on this row work 2 trs in every other dc, single trs in between. This cuts the circumference by a third. It might be a good idea to do the "small" size this way in any event.)

Color stripes: Be prepared to fudge a bit at the back seam from here on. You may not have exactly the same number of stitches in Row 20 as I did so that fancy-stitch rows may not always end evenly. If this happens, just skip a stitch or work two in one to make up the difference.

Row 21: Do not turn. Attach C to hook, * draw up a loop in each of the next 2 trs of Row 20, yo, draw through all loops on hook, ch 1. Rep from * around, sl st in first st, break off. Turn.

Row 22: With D, sc in a ch 1 space, * insert hook in next st, yo, draw through a loop, yo, draw through 2 loops on hook, rep twice more from * in same st, yo, draw through 3 loops on hook, yo, draw through last 2. "Pop" st made. Sc in ea ch 1 sp and "pop" st in each st around, sl st in 1st sc, break off, turn.

Row 23: With B, sc in each st, sl st in 1st sc, break off. Do not turn.

Row 24: With E, sl st and ch 2 in next sc, dc in the sc behind it. Now skip the next sc after the ch 2, dc in the next sc, then dc in the skipped dc. You should be getting crossed doubles. * Skip next sc, dc in next, dc in skipped sc, rep from * around, sl st in top of end dc, break off. Do not turn.

Row 25: With F, rep Row 23, sl st in 1st sc, break off. Do not turn.

Row 26: With G, * sc and dc in next sc, skip next sc, rep from * around, sl st in 1st sc, break off. Turn.

Row 27: With H, sc in 1st dc, * yo, insert hook in next sc, yo, draw through a loop, then pull it up to make it a long loop, rep twice more from *, yo, draw through all loops on hook, ch 1. This makes a "puff" st with a ch 1 following it. Sc in each dc and puff st and ch 1 in each sc around, sl st in 1st st, break off. Turn.

For the next row, which is an increase row, it is important to note that in the previous row the sc, puff, and ch 1 all constitute individual stitches.

Row 28: With C, sl st and ch 3 in next st * skip 1 st, dc in next, ch 1, rep from * around, sl st in middle ch of ch 3, ch 1, turn. (There should be about a third more stitches than there were in Row 26.)

Row 29: Sc in each dc and in each ch 1 space, sl st in 1st st, break off. Turn.

Row 30: With F, rep Row 21, sl st in 1st st, break off. Turn.

Row 31: With D, sc and dc in each ch 1 space, sl st in 1st st, break off. Turn.

Row 32: With E, sc in 1st dc, * puff st in next (no ch 1 after puff on this row), sc in next dc, rep from * around, sl st in 1st st, break off. Do not turn.

Row 33: With H, rep Row 21, sl st in 1st st, break off. Turn.

Row 34: With G, rep Row 22, sl st in 1st st, break off. Turn.

Row 35: With B rep Row 23, sl st in 1st, break off. Do not turn.

Row 36: Scallop edging. With A, * sc in next sc, skip 2 scs, work 9 trs in next sc, skip 2 scs, rep from * around, sl st in 1st sc, break off, weave in loose ends.

If you want to block the collar, do so by placing a damp cloth over the *wrong* side and just passing a warm iron over it. Do not press down!

Tie: With 2 strands A and the H hook, chain appropriate length for a waistband tie. Press, weave through Row 8 of body, knot ends.

Jacket and Skirt Set

Size:

Directions are for Medium size. Changes for Small and Large sizes are in parentheses.

Jacket: Bust—36″ (32″, 40″) measured closed.

Sleeve length: 19½″ (18″, 21″)—sleeve is long to puff out over cuff.

Sleeve width: 16″ (15″, 17″).

Shoulders (dropped): 6″ (5½″, 6½″).

Underarm to hem: 13″ (12″ to 13″, 14″ to 15″—individual should adjust to desired length.)

Back neck: 6″ (5½″, 6½″).

Materials:

Donegal homespun wool tweed or any comparable weight yarn.

Skirt alone:	approx 16 oz.
Jacket alone:	approx 8 oz.
Entire set:	approx 24 to 25 oz.

Heavyweight mohair or brushed wool for jacket: approx. 11 to 12 oz.

Amounts above are for size Medium. Subtract 1 oz. for size Small; add 2 oz. for size Large

5 Buttons, ¾″ diameter.

Tube elastic—black unless skirt is being made in very light color, in which case use white—about 2 yds.

Hooks:

Sizes I and J aluminum or sizes to obtain gauge.

Gauge:

I (skirt hip ribbing only): tweed yarn, 4 dcs = 1″.

J (skirt dcs): tweed yarn, 3 dcs = 1″.

J (jacket dcs): mohair yarn, 15 dcs = 6″.

6 rows = 4″.

Skirt

Begin at top and work down. With tweed yarn and I hook ch 100 (88, 112).

Hip ribbing:
Row 1: Dc in 3rd ch from hook and in remaining chs 99 (87, 111) dcs counting ch 2 as 1 dc. Ch 1, turn.
Row 2: Skip 1st st, dc around post of next st front (toward you), * dc around post of next at back (away from you), dc around post of next at front, rep from * across row, end with half-double crochet (hdc) in ch at end, ch 1, turn.
Row 3: Skip 1st st, dc around post of next at back, * dc around post of next at front, dc around post of next at back, rep from * across, ending with hdc in ch, ch 1, turn.
Rows 4 through 9: Rep Rows 2 and 3. At end of Row 9, ch 2, turn.
Change to J hook.
Row 10: Dc in 1st dc (next to ch 2), * dc in next dc, 2 dc in next, rep from * across ending with 1 dc in last dc. Should result in 148 (136, 160) sts. Turn.
Row 11: Sl st and ch 2 in 1st dc, dc in ea remaining dc and in ch at end, turn.
Rows 12 through 46 (44, 48) or to desired length: Rep Row 11.
Row 47 (45, 49): Sc in each dc. Block (press) dc section. Sl st back seam tog on wrong side and press.

Waistband: Cut two strips of tube elastic each about 24″ long (21″, 29″) and knot ends of each together to form two circles.
Round 1: With right side facing, sc in each ch around top of skirt, sl st in top of 1st sc, ch 1, turn.
Round 2: Working over one of the circles, sc in ea sc, sl st in 1st sc, ch 1, turn.
Round 3: Sc in 1st sc, * ch 1, skip next sc, sc in next, rep from * around, sl st in 1st sc, ch 1, turn.
Round 4: Rep Round 2.
Round 5: Rep Round 1. Sl st over ea sc, break off, weave in loose ends.

Tie: Ch desired length, press, weave through Round 3, knot ends.

Jacket

Note: Sleeves are added last, worked directly into armholes.

Back: Start at top and work down. With tweed and J hook ch 58 (52, 64).

Shoulder Ribbing:

Rows 1 through 9: Work same as Rows 1 through 9 of skirt but on 57 (51, 63) sts. Break off, turn.

Row 10: With mohair, sl st and ch 2 in 1st dc, dc in next 2 dcs, dec 1 dc over next 2 sts by yo, draw up a loop in ea of next 2 sts, yo, draw through all but last loop on hook, yo, draw through all loops on hook. * Dc in next 3 sts, dec 1 dc over next 2, rep from * across row, turn. Should be 46 (41, 51) sts left.

Rows 11 through 33: Work even in dc as Row 11 of skirt. Shorten or lengthen here. If jacket is made to go with skirt, it should end just below the lower edge of the hip ribbing.

Front: Left-hand side as worn. With tweed and J ch 22 (20, 26).
Rows 1 and 2: As 1 and 2 of back, but on 21 (19, 25) sts.

Neck shaping:

Row 3: Work in rib patt across, end with 2 dcs in last ch, ch 2, turn.

Row 4: Dc in 1st dc, work rest of row in rib patt, ch 1, turn.

Rows 5 through 8: Rep Rows 3 and 4. There should be 27 sts (25, 31).

Row 9: Work even in rib patt. Break off and secure.

Rows 10 through 33: Same as 10 through 33 on back. There will be 22 (20, 25) sts left. Break off.

Right-hand front as worn: With tweed and J ch 22 (20, 26).
Rows 1 and 2: As left side.
Row 3: Dc in 1st dc, work rest of row in rib patt, ch 1, turn.
Row 4: Work in Rib patt across, 2 dcs in last ch, ch 2, turn.
Rows 5 through 8: Rep Rows 3 and 4.
Rows 9 through 33: As left side.

Block all 3 pieces, being careful not to flatten ribbing.

Seams: Join shoulder seams, preferably by slip-stitching them together on the right side. Press. Join side seams between top of 16th (15th, 17th) row down from top and 27th (26th, 28th or as preferred) down from top. Hold pieces together right sides facing so you are working on the wrong side. Sl st the pieces together through the first row, ch 1, sl st the pieces together through the next, ch 1, and so on. This produces a light, flexible seam. Press.

Hem edging: With mohair, right side facing, starting at outer front edge, sc along hem, work 3 scs in corner st to turn, work 2 scs in side of each row to seam, sl st in seam, work around rest of edge in this manner, break off, press. (If it either buckles or fans out, subtract or add stitches where needed to keep it smooth.)

FRONT EDGINGS:

Left-hand (button) side as worn: With tweed and I hook, right side facing, work 2 scs in side of each row, starting with 1 sc in side of sc at hem and ending with last tweed ribbing row before neck curve. Ch 1, turn. Work 5 more rows even in sc, break off.

Right-hand (buttonhole) side: Work to match left, starting at top instead of hem. In Row 4 work buttonholes: Sc in first 2 scs down from top, ch 1, skip 1, * sc in next 9 scs, ch 1, skip 1, rep from * to lower edge, ch 1, turn. In Row 5, sc in each sc and each ch 1 space, work Row 6 even in sc, break off, press both sides. Sew buttons across from buttonholes.

COLLAR:

With tweed and J hook, right side facing, work about 42 (38, 50) scs as evenly as possible around neck edge between front edgings. Ch 1, turn. Work 12 (11, 13) more rows even in sc, increasing 1 sc at each side of every other row, break off. Press.

SLEEVES:

Make two. With mohair and J hook work 43 (39, 47) dcs as evenly as possible around the armhole edge, into the sides of the rows, on a ratio of two to every mohair dc row and one to every tweed rib. Work 27 (25, 29 or desired length) more rows even in dc, break off, turn.

CUFFS:

With tweed and J hook, sl st and ch 2 in the first mohair dc, decrease 1 dc over every 2 sts across row (see Row 10 of back), ch 1, turn. Work 5 (5, 6) more rows even in dc rib pattern, break off. Press sleeve lightly. Close underarm seam in same manner as side seams and press.

Nan Jennes Brown

DAVE SCHERER

Nan Jennes Brown divides her time between designing crocheted items for the country's leading magazines and teaching art to children in the New York City school system. The magazines she designs for include Woman's Day, Woman's Day Needlework and Craft Ideas, Family Circle, Family Circle Fashion & Crafts, Ladies' Home Journal Needle & Craft, Good Housekeeping, and Good Housekeeping Needlecraft. Nan also finds room in her schedule for a crochet club for 6th graders.

"Even though I've been designing professionally for a number of years now, I'm always looking around for new ideas and designs to create. Wherever I travel I like to read and research for new concepts on crochet. The Mon Tricot Knitting Dictionary, a stitches and patterns book which is always being updated and contains more than 1000 different crochet and knitting stitches, is my bible. I have been influenced by many sources and like to give credit when it is deserved. A crocheter and artist, Frank Lincoln Viner, whose designs have appeared in many crochet books, has had perhaps the greatest influence on my work. Frank specializes in tapestry crochet and introduced me to the granite stitch. My tapestry coat that is included in this book is worked in the granite stitch.

"Old books and magazines on crochet, I have found, are a wonderful source of inspiration. Traditional and primitive motifs stimulate design ideas. The tapestry coat was inspired by Mexican motifs; the afghan is a rendering of a traditional quilt pattern. I am receptive to the influences surrounding me; my work often reflects this. My observations and interpretations result in the creation of new designs."

Nan Jennes Brown

Mayan Figure Coat

Size:

Size 7, coat width around underarms, about 4″. To change to other sizes, see notes below.

Materials:

Tweed worsted wool

Blue (A)	8 skeins (4 oz. each)
Orange (B)	5 skeins (4 oz. each)
Yellow (C)	2 skeins (4 oz. each)
Brown (D)	2 skeins (4 oz. each)
Green (E)	1 skein (2 oz.)

1 Skein of brushed wool and mohair yarn (for trim).

Hooks:

Sizes H and I aluminum, or sizes to obtain gauge.

Gauge:

H hook, (sc, ch 1) 2 times = 1″, 7 pattern rows = 2″.

Back: To determine length of starting ch, measure the distance across your back from shoulder to shoulder and add 2″. The chain must be a multiple of 4 plus 3.

Fronts: AREAS A, B, C, D should all correspond in length to back. Make half the increases of the back on each side of front.

Side Panels: Should be between 2½″ and 5″ wide. The width is determined after the back and front have been constructed. Put the finished back and front on in front of mirror and determine width of side for desired fit.

Note: Yarn is worked double for the entire coat.

Length: To make longer coat, add extra rows to AREA A, to blue in AREA B, and to brown in AREA C, as desired, making sure to increase fronts as back.

Changing colors: When changing colors, draw new color through last two loops of last stitch of old color. Always work over strand not in use when working with more than one color. Trim end to 2″ when finished with color and work over the end.

PATTERN STITCH:

Row 1: Work 1 sc in 4th ch from hook, * ch 1, sk 1 ch in next ch, rep from * across; ch 2, turn.

Row 2: Sc in first ch 1 sp of previous row, * ch 1, sc in next ch 1 sp, rep from * across; ch 2, turn.

BACK:

With I hook and A ch 57. Change to H hook. Work in Patt st throughout. 28 patts.

AREA A: Work 8¼″ A. Fasten off A.

AREA B: 4″ Att B, work 2 rows, fasten off. Att C, work 2 rows, fasten off. Att A, work 4 rows, fasten off. Att C, work 2 rows, fasten off. Att B, work 2 rows, fasten off. 12 rows worked.

AREA C: 7″. If you have added stitches to increase the size, work the added stitches at both edges with D to keep block pattern centered.

Attach D. Work 6 rows. With D work (1 sc, ch 1, 1 sc) five times, * with B, (ch 1, 1 sc) four times, with D, (ch, 1 sc) two times, rep * twice more, complete row with D. Work 3 rows B over B and D over D. Fasten off A. Work 6 rows in D. Fasten off D. 21 rows worked.

AREA D (Figure): Attach A. Work any necessary increases at both sides of figure to keep it centered. Work 3 rows. Follow graph on page 65 for figure. Work 8 rows A after figure. Fasten off. Area D measures 20″ long.

FRONTS:

With A and I hook ch 33.

Row 1: Using H hook sc in 4th ch from hook * ch 1, sk 1 ch, sc in next ch, rep from * across 16 patts, counting sc and ch as 1 patt. AREA A and AREA B correspond in color patt and length to AREA C.

Block Pattern: Attach D. Work 6 rows. Work 6 patts, attach B, (work D under B). Work 4 patts in B, work 6 patts in D. Repeat D over D and B over B for 2 rows.

Row 3: Work 6 patts of D. Fasten off B. Attach A. Work 4 patts

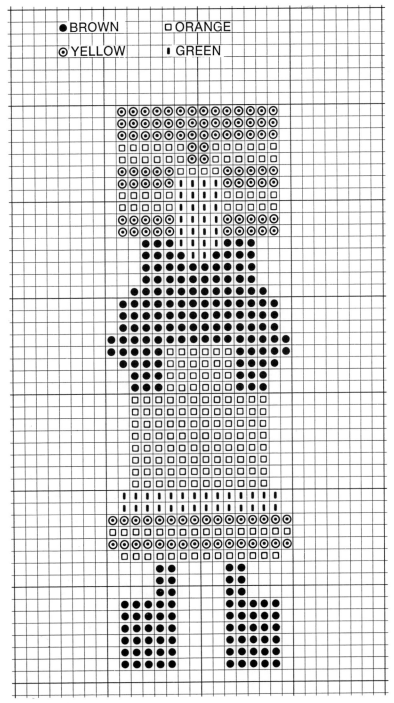

MAYAN FIGURE

in A, 6 patts in D. Rep Row 3 five more times (6 rows). Fasten off A. Work 6 Rows in D.

AREA D: (Correspond to figure on back.) Work 3 rows in A.

Row 4: Work 5 patts in A, attach B (carry in A along), work 4 patts in B, 6 patts in A.

Rows 5 and 6: Work 6 patts in A, 6 patts in B, 5 patts in A.

Row 7: Work 4 patts in A, 1 patt B, 2 patts A, 1 patt B, 5 patts A.

Row 8: 5 Patts A, 1 patt B, 2 patts A, 1 patt B, 4 patts A. Rep Rows 7 and 8 once more.

Row 11: 4 Patts A, 2 patts B, 1 patt A, 1 patt B, 1 patt A, 2 patts B, 5 patt A.

Row 12: Work A to middle B, work B over B, work A to end. Rep Rows 1 through 9 reversing order (Rep Row 9, 8, etc.) Work 4 rows in A.

Next 4 rows: Work 6 patts A, attach C, 4 patts C, 6 patts A. Fasten off C in last row.

Next 6 rows: Work 6 patts A, attach E, 4 patts E, 6 patts A. Fasten off E in last row.

Shape Neck: Dec (by sk 1 sc + work in next sc) 1 sc neck edge for 8 rows. Work on remaining patts for 13 rows. Fasten off. (Front is 2″ longer than back to allow for shoulder.) Make two fronts, reversing neck edge.

Shoulder Seams: Sew together using A, work from shoulder to neck edge. Try on coat and measure desired width of side panel.

Left Side Panel: Right side facing, with B, start with row at top of green block of left front, sc along edge left front, working C about 81 sc to bottom edge. Work even for 4″ or desired width for panel.

Joining Row: Holding right side of back and front tog, work 1 row sc through both pieces. Fasten off. From right side with B, work 1 row sc on top of pick-up row to duplicate effect of joining row.

Right Side Panel: Work to correspond to left side panel.

SLEEVE:

With I hook and A ch 41, join with sl st being careful not to twist the ch.

Round 1: Change to H hook, ch 3 (counts as 1 dc), work 1 dc in each ch around, join with sl st to 3rd ch of starting ch. Working through back loops only, work evenly in dc until 19″ from beg or desired length to underarm. *Note:* both loops for joining with sl st. Fasten off A.

Armhole and Sleeve Joining:

Round 1: From right side with I hook, join A at center of side panel and work sc evenly around armhole. Join with sl st to first sc.

Round 2: Count sc made. Change to H hook, ch 2, using back loop only work 1 hdc in next 2 hdc, dec 1 st over next 2 hdc, work 1 hdc each sc to last 5 dc, dec 1 st over next 2 hdc, work 1 hdc in each of last 3 sc. Join. Continue dec. 1 more hdc row if necessary in order for armhole size to correspond more closely to sleeve size. (Dec evenly around armhole.) Holding wrong side of sleeve to wrong side of coat, sew both pieces together, easing sleeve fullness at top of armhole. Fasten off.

Front Edging:

Row 1: Wrong side facing starting at bottom edge of left front, join A and work 1 row of dc around neck edge with 2 dc in each st at corners of neck shaping to bottom edge of right front.

Row 2: Ch 2, turn, sc in each dc.

COLLAR:

Using B singly with I hook, ch 25, sc in 3rd ch from hook, work 1 sc in each ch, ch 2, turn. Using back loop only sc on each sc, sc into both loops of last sc. Work evenly for 32″ or necessary length for top of coat. Do not break off.

Note: Sew collar to coat starting at beginning of collar; then if you have not worked enough you can continue the collar until it fits the coat. With mohair work 1 row sc up fronts and around collar.

Block coat for good fit. Sew large snaps or flat skirt hooks-and-eyes even to coat to fasten, or use buttons or a large decorative pin.

Child's Jacket

Sizes:

Directions are for size 6. Changes for 8 and 10 are in parentheses.

Materials:

2 4-oz. Skeins hand-dyed or commercial variegated worsted wool, in contrasting solid colors.

4 Buttons, ¾" diameter.

Hook:

Size G aluminum or size to obtain given gauge.

Gauge:

(Sc, ch) five times = 2".
9 pattern rows = 2".
5 Sc = 1", 7 sc rows = 1½".

BACK:

With variegated yarn ch 46 (50, 54).
Row 1: Sc in 4th ch from hook, * ch 1, sk 1 ch, sc in next ch; rep from * across 22 (24, 26) patts counting sc and ch 1 as 1 patt. Ch 2, turn.
Row 2: Sc under first ch 1, * ch 1, sk sc, sc under next ch 1; rep from * across 22 (24, 26) patts. Ch 2, turn. Rep Row 2 for 11½" (12½", 13½") or desired length (allow for a 3" waistband) to shoulder. The Fronts are made in one piece with the back (there are no shoulder seams).
Divide for neck and left front. Work across 6, (8, 10) patts, (do not work remaining sts) for 6 (9, 11) rows.
Row 9: Work across to last ch 1 sp, work (sc, ch 1, sc) in next sp (inc made).
Row 10: Ch 2, turn, work even on 7 patts.
Rows 11 through 22 (24, 26): Rep Rows 1 and 2, inc at neck edge six (eight, ten) more times, 14 (16, 18) patts. Continue working straight for 7½" (8½", 9½"). Fasten off.

RIGHT FRONT:

Skip center 11 patts for back of neck, join variegated yarn and work to correspond to left front, reversing shaping.

Left Side Panel: With right side facing and solid color beginning at bottom of front, work 28, (33, 38) sc to underarm. Ch 2, sc on 28, (33, 38) sc for 1½″ (2″, 21½″). Fasten off.

Right Side Panel: Work to correspond to left side panel.

SLEEVES:

(Attach solid contrasting color at center of side panel at armhole.)

Round 1: Pick up 39 (44, 49), sc around armhole join with sl st. Ch 2.

Round 2: Sc in each sc. join to top of ch 2.

Rounds 3 through 5: Hdc in each sc, dec 1 st each rnd at underarm. Continue in hdc for 14,″ 15,″ 16″ from armhole or desired arm length.

WAISTBAND:

Row 1: Ch 14, sc in 3rd ch from hook, sc to end of ch, ch 2, turn.

Row 2: Using back loop only, sc on 13 (counting ch as 1 sc). Rep Row 2 for 23½″, (25½″, 27½″) or length for bottom of sweater. Fasten off and weave end. Sew to bottom of sweater.

Note: Sew band to jacket starting at beginning of band; then if you have not worked enough you can continue the band until it fits the jacket.

FRONT EDGING:

Row 1: Right side facing, starting at bottom edge right front, attach solid contrasting color and work 1 row of sc around to bottom edge of left front.

Row 2: Ch 2, turn, working back loop only work 1 sc in each sc around, with 3 sc in each sc at corners of neck shaping. Fasten off and weave end.

Row 3: On right front (left front for a boy) use marker for 4 buttonholes evenly spaced, placing 1 at st of V-neck, last 1″ from lower edge and other two in center between them. Work 1 more row of sc working buttonholes at marker.

Buttonhole: Ch 2, sk sc, sc in next st. Fasten off and weave.

Large Victorian Pouch

Materials:

8-cord Ecru cotton twist thread, 5 skeins.

Hook:

Size 00 steel, or size to obtain gauge.

Gauge:

11 dc = 2".

FIRST SECTION:

Start at center, ch 36.

Round 1: Dc in 4th ch from hook, dc in ea of next 33 ch, 5 dc in last ch, working along opposite side of starting ch, dc in next 33 ch, 5 dc in the same place at the bottom of the ch. Join with sl st in top of chain at beg of rnd (77 sts), counting ch at beg of rnd as 1 dc.

Round 2: Ch 2, using back loop only, hdc in next 32 dc, * (2 hdc in the same dc, hdc in the next dc, 3 hdc in next dc, hdc in the next, 2 hdc in the next dc) 33 hdc, rep from * to end, join both loops of 1st hdc.

Round 3: Using back loop only, sc in the next 32 hdc, 2 sc in the next hdc, sc in next 3 hdc, 3 sc in next hdc, sc in next 32 hdc, 2 sc in next hdc, sc in next 33 sc, 2 sc in next, sc in next 2 hdc, 3 sc in next hdc, sc in next 3 hdc, 2 sc in next hdc, join to both loops of 1st sc.

Round 4: Turn to wrong side, ch 2 using back loop only, 2 sc in next sc, sc in next 5 sc, 3 sc in next sc, sc in next 5 sc, 2 sc in next sc, sc in next 33, 2 sc in next sc, sc in next 5 sc, 3 sc in next sc, sc in next 5 sc, 2 sc in next sc, sc in next 32 sc, join to 1st sc using both loops.

Round 5: Working on right side, ch 2, using back loop only, sc in next 32 sc, 2 sc in next sc, sc in next 7 sc, 3 sc in next sc (middle of 3 sc), sc in next 7 sc, 2 sc in next sc, sc in next 33 sc, 2 sc in next sc, sc in next 7 sc, 3 sc in next sc, sc in next 7 sc, 2 sc in next sc, join using both loops, to 1st sc.

Round 6: Work on wrong side, using back loop only, 2 sc in next

71

sc, sc in next 9 sc, 3 sc in next sc, sc in next 9 sc, 3 sc in next sc, sc in next 33 sc, 2 sc in next sc, sc in next 9 sc, 3 sc in next sc, sc in next 9 sc, 2 sc in next sc, sc in next 32 sc, join using both loops to 1st sc.

Round 7: Turn to right side, ch 2, using back loop only sc in next 32 sc, 2 sc in next sc, sc in next 11 sc, 3 sc in next sc, sc in next 11 sc, 2 sc in next sc, sc in next 33 sc, 2 sc in next sc, sc in next 11 sc, 3 sc in next sc, sc in next 11 sc, 2 sc in next sc, join to 1st sc using both loops.

Round 8: Working on right side of section, ch 3, using back loop only, dc in next 33 sts, 2 dc in next dc, dc in next 13 dc, 3 dc in next sc, dc in next 13 sc, 2 dc in next sc, dc in next 33 dc, in next sc work * (2 dc, ch 1, 2 dc), sk 2 sc, sc in next 22 sc, sk 2 sc, rep from *, join.

Round 9: Ch 3 (count as dc), sk dc, dc, wrh, insert hook into next dc * wrh and draw loop up three times, wrh, draw through 6 loops, wrh, draw through 2 loops, ch 1 Pineapple St completed, sk dc, dc on next 2 dc, rep from * seven times, sk next dc, dc on next dc, 3 dc on next dc, rep from * four times, (last * ends with 1 dc), on point work (2 dc, Pineapple St, 2 dc), sk dc, dc in next 2 dc, rep from * three times, (last * ends with 1 dc), 3 dc in next dc, rep from * nine times, sk 2 dc, dc on next dc, on ch 1 work (2 dc, ch 1, 2 dc), dc on sc, sk 2 dc, working loosely, sl st on next 20 sc, sk 2 sc, 2 dc, on ch 1 work (2 dc, ch 1, 2 dc), join with a sl st to the top of ch 3.

Round 10: Ch 3, using back loop only * (dc on ea dc and ch 1), (33 sts), work 3 dc on next st, rep from * 19 sts, 3 dc on next st, rep from * 36 sts, on ch 1 work (2 dc, ch 1, 2 dc,) dc on next 2 sts, sk 2 sc, work 13 sc on back of sl st, sk 2 sc, dc on next 2 sts, on ch 1 work (2 dc, ch 1, 2 dc), dc on next 3 sts, using both loops join with sl st to top of ch 3.

Round 11: Ch 4, * sk dc, dc on next dc, ch 1, rep from * 18 spaces, sk dc, on next dc work (dc, ch 1, dc), ch 1, rep from * 10 spaces, sk dc, work (dc, ch 1, dc) on next dc, rep from * 11 spaces, sk dc, work (dc, ch 1, dc) on next dc, rep from * 20 spaces, sk 2 dc, on ch 1 work (2 dc, ch 1, 2 dc), rep from * 2 spaces, sk 2 sts, sc on 9 sc, sk 2 sts, dc, ch 1, sk 1 st, dc, sk 1 st, on ch 1 work (2 dc, ch 1, 2 dc), (sk dc, dc, ch 1) two times, join to top of ch 3.

Round 12: Ch 3 * dc on ch 1, dc around post of each dc, insert hook, (wrh hook, insert hook in space before next st, bring hook across back of st and out in space after st from back to front) [left-handed crocheter works from front to back] draw through a loop and work off as a dc). Post St completed, rep

from * eighteen times, 3 dc on ch 1, rep from * eleven times, 3 dc on ch 1, rep from * twelve times, 3 dc on ch 1, rep from * twenty-two times, 3 dc on ch 1, rep from * four times, work 11 sc across top, rep from * eight times, join to top of ch 3.

Round 13: Ch 3, * dc in Post St alternating 1 Post St from front to back, next Post St from back to front, rep from * around to sc at top, 11 dc across top, rep from * to end join to top of ch 3. Break off and weave end.

Make 2 more sections the same as the first section.

Joining of sections: Hold two sections with right sides together. Starting at the top corner and working down along side edges, sc evenly through both sections down to center st of bottom curved edge, turn. Pick up third section and hold in front of second section, right sides together. Working to correspond with first seam, join third section to free edge of second section from center of bottom curved edge up to next top corner space. Break off and weave end. Turn. Join free side edge of free side of first section in the same manner. Fasten off and weave end.

Joining lace: Work lace on each joining as follows:
Row 1: Sc on each sc, turn.
Row 2: Sl st in first sc, 2 sc, * ch 4, sk sc, sc on next 2 sc, rep from * to top ending with sl st. Turn.
Row 3: Sl st on each ch 4 work (3 sc, ch 3, 3 sc), sl st. Fasten off and weave end.

TOP:

Attach thread at any joining, ch 3.
Round 1: Dc on each dc around top. Join. Ch 5.
Round 2: Sk dc, dc on next dc, ch, rep * around. Join. Ch 3.
Rounds 3 through 6: Rep Post St as in Round 12 of first section. Alternating 1 Post St from front to back, next Post St from back to front, work around. Join. Ch 2.
Round 7: Sc in each Post St (dc). Join. Break off and weave end.

DRAWSTRING:

Make ch 36" long. Sc in 3rd. ch from hook and in each ch across. Break off and fasten. Weave drawstring through spaces of Round 2 of top. Holding ends tog tie a knot 1" from ends.

TASSEL:

Wind thread about forty times around a 3½″ piece of cardboard; tie at one end; cut at opposite end. Wind and tie
separate strand around tassel ¼″ below tied end. Sew tassel to
bottom of bag. Trim tassel evenly.

Woman's Textured Top

Size:

Directions are for size 8. See note for size change.

Materials:

Black wool worsted (A)	2 oz.
Lavender rayon (B)	100-yd. spool
Purple variegated brushed wool and mohair-type wool (C)	2 oz.
Blue tweed wool (D)	4 oz.
Lavender tweed wool (E)	2 oz.

Hook:

Sizes I and J aluminum, or sizes to obtain gauge.

Gauge:

I hook, 3 dc = 1″; 3 hdc = 1″; 2 rows hdc = 1″.

Note: There is no armhole shaping. The armhole is formed by side panels. A size increase is made by widening the panel. To add length repeat Rows 2 and 3 (inc. 1½″), repeat Rows 6 through 9 (3 rows = 1″). Repeat Rows 28 through 30 (3 rows = 1″).

FRONT:

With J hook and color A ch 36 (10¼″). Change to I hook.

Row 1: Dc in 3rd ch from hook, dc in each ch (35 dc) counting turning ch as dc, ch 2, turn.

Row 2: Dc in each dc, ch 2, turn.

Row 3: Dc around post of each dc (wrh hook, insert hook in space before next st, bring hook across back of st and out in space after st from back to front, draw through a loop and work off as a dc), ch 2, turn.

Row 4: Dc in each dc, ch 3, turn.

Row 5: Attach B and knot threads. Fasten off A. Rep Row 3, ch 2, turn.

Rows 6 through 9: Sc in each st. Attach C and fasten off B.

Row 10: With C and right side facing, hdc in next 2 sc, * hdc in next st 2 rows below (draw up loop so work doesn't pucker), (hdc bar st completed), hdc bar at 3 rows below next st, hdc bar st 2 rows below next st, hdc in next 3 sc, rep * across ending with 4 hdc. (Count sts each time a hdc bar st row is completed, because it is easy to pick up extra sts, 35 sts), ch 2, turn.

Row 11: Hdc in each st across. Attach D in the last st, fasten off C. Ch 2, turn.

Row 12: Hdc in each hdc across. Ch 2, turn.

Row 13: Hdc in each hdc picking up the front loop only. Ch 2, turn.

Row 14: Hdc in each hdc, picking up back loop only. Ch 2, turn.

Row 15: Rep Row 13. Attach E, fasten off D, ch 2, turn.

Row 16: Rep Row 10.

Row 17: Rep Row 15.

Row 18: Picking up back loop only, sc in next st, (sc, ch 3, sl st in front part of last sc worked) Picot st completed, * sc in next 3 sts, ch 3, picot rep * across to end, sc in last sts. Attach D, do not fasten off E, ch 2, turn.

Row 19: Sc across row, pushing picots to right side of work, ch 2, turn.

Row 20: Sc in next sc, picot, * 2 sc, picot, rep * across. Pick up E, ch 2, fasten off D. Turn.

Row 21: Rep Row 19.

Rows 22 through 25: Rep Rows 15 and 16, 2 times. Attach C and ch 2, at end of Row 25. Fasten off E.

Rows 26 and 27: Rep Rows 10 and 11. Attach B, ch 2.

Row 28 through 30: Sc across. Attach A at end of Row 30 and fasten off B, ch 2, turn.

Row 31: Sc across.

BACK:

Rep Rows 1 through 31.

SIDE PANEL:

Row 1: Using D and I hook pick up 38 sc along side of front, ch 2.

Row 2: Sc across. Ch 2, turn.

Rows 3 through 7: Hdc in each sc. Working on wrong side, sc side panel to back. Work other side panel to correspond.

Work 1 rnd of D in hdc around completed top, 8 hdc on each side panel, join to 1st st and fasten off.

STRAPS:

Front side facing, Attach D to the 6th st from the end of front section, ch 2 (count as 1 hdc), hdc in next 5 sts. Work on 6 hdc for 28 rows or to desired strap length (remember the straps will stretch a little). Fasten off and attach to back section on the wrong side. Work other strap to correspond to first.

NECK EDGE:

Attach B and ch 2.

Round 1: Work 1 rnd of hdc across neck front, along sides of strap, across neck back and along side of second strap. Attach C and fasten off B. Ch 2.

Round 2: Hdc in each hdc. Attach A and fasten off C. Ch 2.

Round 3: Sc in next hdc, picot st in next hdc, * sc in next 2 hdc, picot st in next hdc, rep * around, join with a sl st to top of ch 2.

ARMHOLE AND BOTTOM EDGE:

Using A rep Rnd 3.

Afghan

"Barn Raising" formed by arrangement of "Log Cabin" blocks.

Size:

Approx 5′6″ by 5′6″.

Materials:

12 oz. for center square.
12 oz. for outside border.

Leftover yarns are perfect for this afghan. I used worsted-weight wool; however, synthetic yarns or sports yarn can also be used for this project. Total weight is 3½ lbs.

Hook:

Size H aluminum or size to obtain gauge.

Gauge:

14 dc = 4″, 4 rows = 2″.

Note: Each square begins with 2 rows of granny square using one basic color. It is important to plan the color combination of each square before crocheting it. Four light colors are worked on two sides (side triangle), and four dark colors on the other two sides. Always begin with the light color, then alternate dark, light, dark, etc. I suggest that you plan the following group of squares with similiar color combinations. Please see diagram on page 82.

AREA A—center motif—4 squares with the *exact same* color combination.
AREA B—12 squares with similar color scheme.
AREA C—20 squares with similar color scheme.
AREA D—28 squares with similar color scheme.

Total squares for afghan—64.

D	D	D	D	D	D	D	D
D	C	C	C	C	C	C	D
D	C	B	B	B	B	C	D
D	C	B	A	A	B	C	D
D	C	B	A	A	B	C	D
D	C	B	B	B	B	C	D
D	C	C	C	C	C	C	D
D	D	D	D	D	D	D	D

DARK SIDE   LIGHT SIDE

CENTER SQUARE:

(Granny) With main color, ch 5, join with a sl st to form a ring.

Round 1: Ch 3 (counts as first dc), in ring work 2 dc, ch 1; (3 dc, ch 1, 3 dc) 3 times, join to top of ch 3 with a sl st. (Always join rounds in this manner.)

Round 2: Ch 3, 2 dc in the same place (half corner), * ch 1, 3 dc, ch 1, 3 dc in the next space (corner), rep from * around; end ch 1, 3 dc in last sp (half corner). Ch 1, join. Fasten off.

SIDE TRIANGLE 1:

Attach light color in any corner of center square, ch 3.

Row 1: Working along 1 side edge. * dc on each dc and ch 1 of square, (8 dc), on corner ch 1, work (2 dc, ch 1, 2 dc), rep. * to ch 1 at end of second side (8 dc). Break off.

Attach dark color in last loop of light color st work (knot 2 ends), ch 3, dc on side of light dc, dc in each dc plus ch 1 to corner (10 dc), (2 dc, ch 1, 2 dc) in corner, rep * across remaining free side of square (8 dc), work 2 dc across side of light dc (10 dc). Break off.

Continue building up triangles, inc 2 dc each side of triangle (4 dc triangle), alternating light colors on 3, 5, 7 triangles, dark colors on 4, 6, and 8th triangle for each square.

Weave the loose ends through the wrong side at the completion of each square. Assemble the squares on the floor according to the diagram.

Hint: Taking an instant picture or looking through the viewer of a camera helps to see how the colors of each square look next to each other.

Sew squares together as shown on diagram.

BORDER:

Dc around completed afghan (2 dc, ch 1, 2 dc in corners) for 4".

Judith Copeland

On Manhattan's East 53rd Street, in the shadow of the impressive new Citicorp Center, is Judith Copeland's Quickit, an impressive yarn emporium well known to New York's most sophisticated crocheters and knitters. When not in her shop dispensing mohair, angora, or words of needlework wisdom, Judith is usually off somewhere busily designing creative garments for major magazines such as American Home Crafts, Ladies' Home Journal Needle & Craft, Family Circle, and Woman's Day, or thinking up innovative garment constructions like those found in her new book, Modular Crochet.

A native of Detroit, Judith once designed crochet garments for a leading New York knitwear company and set up a business and training program in Barbados that eventually employed three hundred people. Her designs from this period were retailed in such top stores as Henri Bendel, Bloomingale's, and Saks Fifth Avenue. Her work has also been featured in the pages of Mademoiselle, Glamour, Harper's Bazaar, and Vogue.

"Not long after I first opened my shop I began to listen to some of the things my customers would say as they leafed through instruction books and magazines. Often they were upset when they couldn't find a garment with exactly the right style, or they would comment that something was attractive but its sleeves were too short or too long. At the same time my European customers, those who were trained in knitting and crochet from childhood, would look at the same instructions and figure out how to make whatever changes they wanted. A lot of Americans, it seemed to me, were terrified at the prospect of having to change any part of a garment. This started me thinking about devising simple garment-making techniques that would be easy for beginners.

"First, I took existing patterns straight from books and magazines and encouraged my customers to substitute yarns to put stripes into solid-colored garments, to mix yarns and do other things to alter the instructions. Then I began rewriting existing instructions so that someone following them had the maximum opportunity to be creative; instead of being full of step-by-step specifics, these patterns were full of options. This finally led to my designing original garments that were so simple that the only thing left in the instructions, besides the measurements for the simple shapes involved, were the options—what yarn to use, what gauge, what stitches, what colors were all left up to the crocheter. My customers have had a lot of success with these patterns, and many of them now design their own garments almost exclusively. Now it's hard to tell my American customers from the Europeans."

Judith Copeland

Modular Crochet: How to Make Your Own Custom Design Pullovers from Four Rectangles

Many crocheters, after they have become more experienced at their craft and can follow instructions better, would like to know how to plan a garment so that they can work out ideas of their own. They may have a particular yarn they want to use, or a current style they would like to work up, but can't because the right instructions are not to be found. Sometimes these problems can be solved by substituting the yarn in existing instructions and/or altering instructions in one way or another to get the desired styling. If neither of these alternatives is possible the next solution is to custom design the garment right from the beginning. For most fledgling designers, however, the thought of designing on their own is overwhelming because they do not know where or how to start. In a situation like this the easiest solution is the best solution and that is to make the garment from rectangles.

Working with rectangles avoids many countings of stitches, increasing and decreasing to get the right fit and styling, and elaborate detailing to finish off the garment. The kind of styling that results when garments are made from rectangles is most satisfying. In terms of function, they are comfortable and easy to maintain. In terms of the lines, they are clean and flowing. The overall look is streamlined.

When garments are made from rectangles the procedure is simple and direct. After choosing a yarn and stitch a chain is made to the desired width of the piece or front. The piece is then worked straight up until the desired length is reached. The back is made in the same way. The front and back are then sewn together at the shoulders and the garment is folded in half. The side seams are sewn in until the sleeve opening is the size you want the width of the sleeve to be. The sleeve is crocheted onto the main piece at the armhole and it is then worked to the desired length. All of this is so easy even beginners can turn out sophisticated garments.

The following project describes one kind of systematic approach that can be taken when designing pullovers made from rectangles. All pullovers are made from:

a. a basic set of instructions; the basic pullover instructions,
b. the basketweave stitch; a single crochet and a chain 1,
c. four rectangles (rectangle 1 is the front, rectangle 2 is the back, rectangle 3 is the left sleeve, rectangle 4 is the right sleeve.)

The basic pullover instructions are used as a general working guide. They tell you how to make four rectangles in the basketweave stitch and how to put them together. The other decisions are made by you. They include choosing:

a. the yarn or yarns,
b. the hook size,
c. the width and length of the rectangles.

What you decide to do is what will give each pullover its special styling and silhouette. Here are just a few of many possibilities. Work the rectangles short and narrow in one color and a plain yarn to make a body-hugging pullover. Work medium width rectangles alternating two rows each of two different textured yarns to make a pullover that will rest lightly on the curves of the body. Work the rectangles wide and long in different width stripes of several colors to make a pullover that will hang loose and free.

If you need help determining the right size hook or yarn amounts any reputable yarn shop will be able to give you advice.

Basic Pullover
Instructions

FRONT:

Work a ch to desired width.

Row 1: Work 1 sc in 3rd ch from hook. * Ch 1. Skip 1 ch. Work 1 sc in next ch. Rep from * until piece is desired width ending the row with a sc stitch. Ch 1, turn. If you do not use all of the chains the extra chains can be removed by inserting a hook into the last chain and pulling them out one at a time.

Next Rows: Work 1 sc arnd first ch 1. * Ch 1. Work 1 sc arnd next ch 1. Rep from * across. Make last sc of row in top of last sc of previous row. Ch 1, turn. Rep until piece is desired length. Cut yarn, fasten.

BACK:

Work same as front.

Shoulder Seam: With right side of fabric facing you place front and back together at the shoulder. Starting at outer edge and matching corresponding stitches, sew the seam with a whip stitch under the two loops of each stitch, on each side, until desired neck opening is reached. Repeat procedure for other side. Make adjustments if necessary. Cut yarn, fasten.

Side Edging: On right side of fabric, at bottom side edge, pull a loop arnd the end stitch of the first row. Ch 2. * Skip 1 row. Work 1 sc arnd end st of next row. Ch 1. Rep from * along entire side edge. Cut yarn, fasten. Rep procedure along other side edge.

Note: If you decide at this point that you would like more width to your garment you can add extra rows to each side edging as we did in the mixed yarn pullover.

Side Seams: Fold the garment in half at the shoulders so that the right side of the fabric is facing you. Starting at side bottom edge sew the seam with a whip stitch as described in Shoulder Seam until sleeve opening is desired width. Repeat procedure for other side seam.

Neck Trim: Pull a loop through a ch 1 opening, ch 1. * Work a ch into next ch opening, ch 1. Rep from * arnd entire neck edge. Cut yarn, fasten.

Bottom Trim: At bottom edge of front pull a loop arnd a ch 1 of first row at side seam. Ch 2. * Work 1 sc arnd next ch 1. Ch 1. Rep from * arnd entire bottom. Cut yarn, fasten.

SLEEVES:

With wrong side of stitch facing you and starting at armhole bottom, pull a loop arnd the first stitch, ch 2. Work 1 sc arnd next ch 1. * Ch 1, Work 1 sc arnd next ch 1. Rep from * arnd. At end, ch 1, turn. Next Rows: Work stitches as before until sleeve is desired length. Cut yarn, fasten.

Side Edging: Work Side Edging along entire edge on each side of sleeve.

Seams and Trim: Work same as for body of pullover.

The following designs show three different ways in which the basic pullover instructions can be customized in order to get special effects. In making your pullover you can follow the instructions exactly or the instructions can be used to give you ideas on how to go about developing your own designs.

The pullovers are worked up into three different widths and lengths so you can see how rectangles of different sizes affect the styling and silhouette. The first pullover is made from narrow rectangles to make it fit close to the body. It is short. Ending at the waist, the top is the smallest part of the outfit. This gives the full figure a ¼–¾ proportion that results in a long-legged look.

The second pullover is wider. The extra width makes a looser garment and the results are straight lines; streamlined styling. Worked a little longer the proportions are now ⅓–⅔ and they still give a long-legged look.

The third pullover is the same width but worked longer; it covers the hips. The proportions have been reversed to ⅔–⅓. Now the top garment is the largest part of the outfit so it predominates over the full figure. These kinds of proportionings will give you a long lean line rather than ½–½ proportioning which tends to cut the body in half.

To make the pullovers shown here follow the basic pullover instructions. Refer to the following customized instructions for information on yarn type, chain length, color changes, and so on.

Striped Pullover

Size:

Directions are for Small (bust 30″ to 32″). Changes for Medium (34″ to 36″) and Large (38″ to 40″) are in parentheses.

Materials:

Natuurwol (natural wool) from Holland, or a comparable sport-weight wool yarn, 145-yard skeins, 4 (5, 6) skeins:

Dark Brown (A)
Medium Brown (B)

Hook:

Size G aluminum, or size to obtain gauge.

Gauge:

1 sc and 1 ch = ½″.

STRIPE PATTERN:

* Work 2 rows of color B to last stitch. Drop B and pick up A to make the last loop of the last stitch. Ch 1, turn. Work 2 rows of color A to last stitch. Drop A and pick up B to make the last loop of the last stitch. Ch 1, turn. Rep from * throughout. Put another way, in the last row of a color, the last loop of the last stitch is made in the other picked-up color. To get a neat, uniform edge always pick the yarn up in the same way and don't pull it too loose or too tight.

FRONT AND BACK:

Row 1: Following the Basic Pullover Instructions, with color A, work the ch and Row 1 to 15″ (16″, 17″).
Row 2: Work to last sc. Dropping A make the last loop of the last sc in color B. Ch 1, turn.

Next Rows: Changing colors every 2 rows as described above, work the rectangles to a length of 16″ (17″, 18″) or to desired length.

Side Edging: Work in color A.

Side Seams: Leave an armhole opening of 6″ (6½″, 6½″). for the sleeve.

SLEEVES:

Work 6″ (6½″, 6½″) wide and to desired length.

Side Edging: Work in color A.

STRIPED PULLOVER

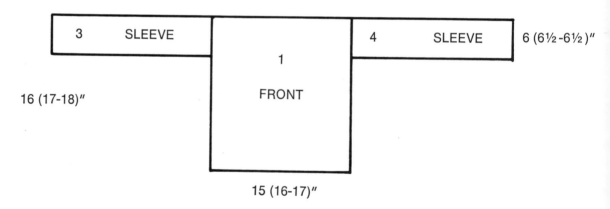

Bulky Yarn Pullover

Materials:

Bulky-weight wool, 119-yard skeins, 8 (9, 10) skeins Natural.

119-yard skeins, 8 (9, 10) skeins.

Hook:

Size J aluminum or size to obtain gauge.

Gauge:

3 sc and 3 ch 1 = 2″.

FRONT AND BACK:

Following the Basic Pullover Instructions work the ch and Row 1 to 19″ (20″, 21″). Work the rectangles to a length of 20″ (22″, 24″) or to desired length. Work Side Edgings as described.

Side Seams: Leave an armhole opening of 6½″ (7″, 7″) for the sleeve.

SLEEVES:

Work 6½″ (7″, 7″) wide and to desired length.

BULKY YARN PULLOVER

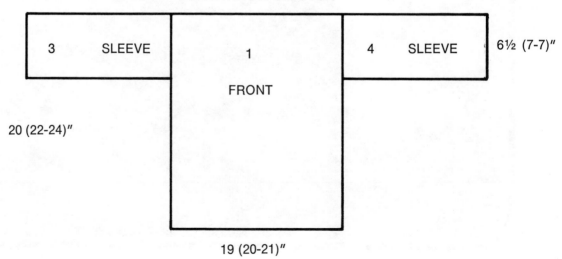

Mixed Yarn Pullover

Materials:

Lightweight Alpaca, 165-yard skeins, 8 (9, 10) skeins each:
Dark Brown (A)
Medium Brown (B)

Hook:

Size J aluminum or size to obtain gauge.

Gauge:

1 sc and 1 ch = ½".

FRONT AND BACK:

With 1 strand of A and B held together follow the Basic Pullover Instructions working the ch and Row 1 to 18" (19", 20"). Work the rectangles to a length of 22" (24", 26") or to desired length.

MIXED YARN PULLOVER

3	SLEEVE		1 FRONT	4	SLEEVE

6 (6½-6½)"

20 (22-24)"

SIDE EDGING   SIDE EDGING

1½"

BOTTOM TRIM

1"   18 (19-20)"   1"

Side Edgings: For a different effect make a wider border on each side of the rectangles by working 4 rows of edging rather than 1.

Side Seams: Leave an armhole opening of 6″ (6½″, 6½″) for the sleeve.

Bottom Trim: Work 7 rows for a wide border.

SLEEVES:

Work 6″ (6½″, 6½″) wide and to desired length.

Note: If you want to wear a long pullover with a shorter vest, tie the pullover at the waist and pull the garment up into an overlap or blouse.

How to Make a Vest from Three Rectangles

The vest, like the pullover is also made of rectangles. And again, you can use any yarn or yarns you wish. The same yarn, such as a smooth maroon wool, can be used throughout for a plain look. You can mix several kinds as done here to make a more extravagant garment, or stripe it. Whatever your design, just work your chain and rectangles to the sizes indicated.

About Mixed Yarns: If you decide to work with mixed yarns it gives you the opportunity to custom design a fabric in the way that a weaver does. In this technique two or more strands are held together and they are worked the same as a single strand. If you work at a medium tension without forcing the stitches it is no more difficult than working with a single strand. You can work the entire vest in the same combination of yarns or you can change the combination whenever you like. If yarns are changed throughout a piece any number of strands can be combined as long as each combination is approximately the same thickness. This way the gauge or the density of the fabric will be maintained throughout. For instance, to maintain thickness the combination might consist of only 1 thick yarn and 1 thin yarn, or as many as 6 strands if all the yarns are thin.

Vest

Sizes:

Directions are for Small size (bust 30″, 32″). Changes for Medium (34″ to 36″) and Large (38″, 40″) are in parentheses.

Finished Measurements:

Width of Back 19″ (20″, 21″). Width of each Front 9½″ (10″, 10½″).

Materials:

Bulky-weight wool (119-yard skeins), 5 (6, 7) skeins.
Hand-spun Mexican wools (120-yard skeins), 2(3, 4) skeins.
Various medium- and lightweight yarns in different colors and textures 14 (15, 16) ozs.

We used several types of wools in natural colors, nubbly tweeds, and thick and thin multi-colored handspun wools from Mexico and Colombia. A project such as this offers the perfect opportunity to use up scrap wools. All in all you will need approximately 2 (2¼ to 2½) lbs. of yarn.

Hook:

Size 16 wood hook or size to obtain gauge. If you are using another yarn or yarns and a different size hook, a reputable yarn shop can recommend the yarn amounts needed.

Gauge:

3 sc = 2″.

BACK:

Leaving a tail of 6½″, with your yarn or yarns, work a ch to 19″ (20″, 21″).
Row 1: Work 1 sc in 3rd ch from hook and in each ch across until piece measures 19″ (20″, 21″). If you do not use all of the chains the extra chains can be removed by inserting a hook into the last chain and pulling them out one at a time.

Next Rows: * Work 1 sc in each sc across. Ch 1, turn. Rep from
* until piece measures 20″ (22″, 24″) or to desired length. Cut
yarn, fasten. In our vest we changed to a new combination of
yarns at the end of every 2 rows.

LEFT FRONT:

Count the amount of stitches in last row of back. Leaving an
end thread of 6½″ chain half the amount of stitches just
counted. Work same as back. Although this isn't necessary, for
our vest we used the same combination of yarns for every 2
rows as in the back.

RIGHT FRONT:

Work same as left front.

Shoulder Seams: Place back and left front together at the
shoulders. Starting at the outer edge and matching corresponding stitches, sew the seam with a whip stitch under the
2 top loops of each stitch, on each side, for 5½″ (6″, 6½″) or
until piece fits comfortably at the neck. Repeat for other
shoulder seam.

Fringe: Holding several strands of yarn together cut the fringes
into 17″ lengths. Use enough strands to make a fairly bulky
fringe. When using mixed yarns change the combination of
yarns occasionally so the fringes won't all be the same. The
amount of fringes you will need depends on the length of the
vest so just cut up a few at a time.

Side Joining: The front is joined to the back with a fringe.
Starting at bottom side edge fold the 17″ length of fringe in half
to form a loop. Slip the looped end around the end stitch of the
first row of both the front and the back. Pull the loose ends
through the loop. Pull the 6½″ end threads through the same
loop. Pull the fringe ends gently to tighten. Working along side
edge work one fringe around the end stitch of every other row
stopping 10″ short of top edge to allow for the armhole
opening. Repeat the same procedure for the other side edge.

Fringe Trim: Tie a fringe around the end stitch of every other
row along the front edges and the armhole edges. Remember to
slip the 6½″ end threads into the fringe. Tie a fringe around
every other stitch around the neck. Trim fringe ends if
necessary.

Mittens

Sizes:

Directions are for Small size. Changes for Medium and Large are in parentheses.

Finished Measurements:

7" (7½", 8") around mitten.

Materials:

Lightweight Alpaca (165-yard skeins), 1 skein each of Dark Brown (A) and Camel (B), or any suitable yarn that will give the gauge.

Hook:

Size E aluminum or size to obtain gauge.

Gauge:

5 sc = 1".

START:

Starting at fingertips with color A, ch 3. Join with a slip stitch into first ch to form a ring.

Round 1: Work 7 sc into ring. Work 8th sc making last loop of stitch in color B. Drop color A.

Round 2: Continuing with B, work 2 sc in each sc arnd making last loop of last sc in A. Drop B. Total 16 sc.

Round 3: * With A work 1 sc in first sc, work 2 sc in next sc. Rep from * arnd making last loop of last sc in B. Drop A. Total 24 sc.

Round 4: * With B work 1 sc in next 2 sc. Work 2 sc in next sc. Rep from * arnd making last loop of last sc in A. Drop B. Total: 32 sc.

Round 5: Work this rnd for size med and large only. * With A work 1 sc in next 3 sc. Work 2 sc in next sc. Rep from * (2–4) times. Then work 1 sc in each sc arnd making last loop of last sc in B. Drop A. Total (35 to 37) sc.

Next Rounds: Alternating 1 row each of A and B, work 1 sc in each sc. Work mitten to thumb. Cut yarn just used in last rnd.

Thumbhole Opening: Picking up the uncut yarn, ch 8 (9, 10). Skip 8 (9, 10) sc. Work 1 sc in each sc arnd and in each ch for thumb opening working last loop of last sc of rnd in cut yarn.

Next Rounds: Continue as before until mitten is 7" from thumb or to desired length. Try the mitten on as you work along. If it gets too tight increase 1 sc every other rnd or so to get the right fit. Cut yarn and fasten.

Thumb:

Round 1: With next color pull a loop through top loop of first stitch at corner of thumb opening. Work 19 (20, 21) sc arnd making last loop of last sc in other color.

Rounds 2 through 6: Alternating colors, work 1 sc in each sc arnd.

Rounds 7 through 15 (16, 17): Work 1 sc in each sc arnd making a dec of 1 (pull loop up in next sc, pull loop up in next sc, yo hook and pull through all 3 loops on hook) in every other rnd.

Last 2 Rounds: Work the dc st arnd to close thumb opening. Cut yarn, fasten.

Hat

Sizes:

Directions are for Small size. Changes for Medium and Large are in parentheses.

Materials:

Rygja wool (100-yard skeins), 2 skeins Natural, or any yarn or combination of yarns that will give the gauge.

Hook:

Size P aluminum or 16 wood hook, or size to obtain gauge.

Gauge:

3 sc = 1½".

Note: Mark the last stitch in each round with a pin. As each round is completed move the pin up to the last stitch. At the end of each round do not turn work to other side or join; just continue working around on the same side.

START:

Starting at top, ch 4. Join with a slip stitch into first ch to form a ring.

Round 1: Work 6 sc into ring.

Round 2: Continuing to work on same side, work 2 sc in each sc arnd. Total 12 sc.

Round 3: * Work 1 sc in next sc. Work 2 sc in next sc. Rep from * arnd. Total 18 sc.

Round 4: * Work 1 sc in next 2 sc. Work 2 sc in next sc. Rep from * arnd. Total: 24 sc.

Round 5: * Work 1 sc in next 3 sc. Work 2 sc in next sc. Rep from * arnd. Total 30 sc.

Round 6: * Work 1 sc in next 4 sc. Work 2 sc in next sc. Rep from * 2 (3–4) times. Work 1 sc in each sc to end of rnd. Total: 33 (34–35) sc.

Next Rounds: Work 1 sc in each sc until hat reaches bottom of ear. *Turn work to reverse side.*

Brim:
Next Rounds: Work 1 sc in each sc until hat measures 13″ from crown to bottom or to desired length.

Del Pitt Feldman

MALCOLM VARON

When the history of crochet and its phenomenal growth in the 1960s and 1970s is written, a chapter will have to be devoted to Del Pitt Feldman and her shop-gallery-school, Studio Del, on New York's East 7th Street, which became the gathering place for a large number of creative young crocheters and a showplace for their innovative works. And the bibliography of that history of crochet will have to include both of Del's very successful books Crochet: Discovery and Design and The Crocheter's Art. Her work has been shown at New York's Museum of Contemporary Crafts and featured in the American Craft Council's Craft Horizons magazine. She has exhibited at Julie: Artisans' Gallery and at The Elements, two of the finest craft galleries in the country. She is a regular contributor of designs to Ladies' Home Journal Needle & Craft, and notable wearers of Del's imaginative crocheted costumes include Cher, Lily Tomlin, and the 5th Dimension.

"I've always encouraged crocheters to use unusual materials in their work. I believe that if you can wrap something around your crochet hook, you should try crocheting with it. Try a strand of licorice; if it doesn't work, you can always eat it. I once found some marvelous plastic material while rummaging through a warehouse and used it to crochet a stage costume for Janis Joplin. It crocheted up very well and the material it made was beautifully translucent. In the crochet I combined all kinds of found objects and bells that really sparkled and glittered in the stage lights. That was one of my most successful theatrical pieces.

"The theater itself gives me ideas for designs, especially historical theater. My husband, George, is an opera freak—he says buff—and when we go to the Met to see Tosca or La Traviata or some other opera, he listens and I listen and also think of things to crochet. My interest in history is always showing up in my work. The bed jacket in ribbon was inspired by the Victorian period; the medieval fantasy coat was inspired by a trip to the Metropolitan Museum of Art.

"Sometimes I make things that are very simple in design, and then the yarn becomes the most important thing in the garment. But when I have a particularly elaborate design in mind, I choose a yarn that will enhance the design, not detract from it. This is important to consider, whether you're working with yarn or something unusual . . . like licorice maybe."

Del Pitt Feldman

Lace Collar and Cuffs

Materials:

Knit cro-sheen, thin weight, 2 skeins.

Hook:

Size 2 steel hook.

COLLAR:

Row 1: Ch 14, dc back into 6th ch from hook, * ch 1, sk 1 and dc in next st, rep from * ending with dc, ch 4, turn.

Row 2: Work dc into next dc and continue in pattern of ch 1, sk 1, dc until 100 rows are completed. End with dc, turn.

Row 101: Dec (by slip stitching to next dc) and work pattern to end. Continue in this manner, dec to next dc st at the same end until 2 dcs are left. Break off. Pick up at other end of band and work the point in the same manner.

Ruffle:

Row 1: Count down (starting at 6 bar row) to 32 rows, attach yarn at top of bar * ch 10 sc into bar, ch 10, sc into next bar, rep from *, until 30 bars have been completed, ending with ch 4, dc into last bar, turn.

Row 2: * Ch 10, sc into center of ch 10, repeat from * ending same as row 1. Repeat Row 2 three more times.

Row 6: Work 6 ch, sl st back to 3rd ch (picot) ch 6, sl st back to 3rd ch (picot) ch 3. Work chain and picot to end. Break off. Work another shorter ruffle in same manner, pick up at same point as other ruffle, working sc in between bars on same row. Work 2 rows of 10 chains and on third row work picot chain.

CUFFS:

Make two. Start same as band on collar but work for 30 rows, make points and break off. Work ruffle in same manner but on longer ruffle make one row shorter.

Blue Stitch Shell Bag

Materials:

4 oz. Thin Aqua corde, or any filled-in, dressy round cord.

Hook:

Size I aluminum or size to give gauge.

Gauge:

3 sc = 1″, 5 sc rows = 2″.

BAG:

Make two pieces. Beg at center top, ch 4.

Row 1: Sc in 2nd ch from hook, 4 sc in next ch, sc in last ch, ch 1, turn (6 sc).

Row 2: Working through back loop of sts only, sc in first 2 sc, 2 sc in next sc, place marker, 2 sc in next sc, sc in last 2 sc, ch 1, turn.

Row 3: Working through back loop of sts only, sc in each sc to within 1 sc of marker, 2 sc in next sc, sl marker, 2 sc in next sc, sc in each sc to end, ch 1, turn 10 sc. Rep Row 3 for rib pattern. Work 13 rows more, ending last row ch 3, turn.

Bag shell pattern:

Row 1: Ch 3 (turning ch counts as first dc), * sk 1 st, working through back loop of stitch in next st work 2 dc, ch 1, 2 dc (shell), sk 1 st, dc in next st, rep from * to end, ch 3, turn.

Row 2: * Work 2 dc into ch 1 of shell ch 1, 2 dc, yo, insert hook from back to front and again to back arnd stem of next dc, draw loop through, complete as a dc (called BPdc), rep from * end dc in top of turning ch, ch 3, turn.

Row 3: * Work shell into next ch 1, yo, insert hook from front to back and again to front arnd post of single dc, draw loop through, complete as a dc (called FPdc), rep from * end dc in top of turning ch, ch 3, turn.

Row 4: * Arnd ch 1 of shell work 3 dc, ch 1, 3 dc, BPdc arnd

post of next dc, rep from * end dc in top of turning ch, ch 3, turn.

Row 5: * Arnd ch 1 of shell work 3 dc, ch 1, 3 dc, FPdc arnd post of next dc, repeat from *, ch 3, turn.

Row 6: Rep Row 4 and fasten off.

Finishing: Being careful to match patterns, pin the 2 parts of bag tog along sides and lower edge. Join yarn to edge of bag. Working through both pieces sc evenly along side edge, along lower point edge, and along other side. Fasten off. If desired, line bag with taffeta or China silk and set zipper with top opening as wide as you wish. Use curtain tassel or antique ornament at point.

Fantasy Coat

Materials:

Double-weight worsted wool yarn:

Black	8 skeins
Teal	5 skeins
Red	4 skeins
Navy	10 skeins

Odd collection of old memorabilia, such as pieces of jewelry, old lace, French paste buttons.

1 ½ yds. of ½″ Velvet ribbon.
4″-wide Lace, 3 yds. long.

Some bits of stuffing material for appliquéd diamond and round shapes.

Felt for lining epaulets.

This coat can be made as a very simple coat by following the instructions for the background only. If you would like to embellish you can work the rest of instructions and also add some of your own innovations as well. By all means, have fun with it and do your own thing.

Materials for Embellishment of Velvet Forms:

G hook.
Cut velvet:

Dusty Pink	3 skeins
Aqua	2 skeins
Hot Pink	1 skein
Royal Blue	1 skein

Hooks:

Sizes G and I aluminum, or sizes to obtain gauge.

Gauge:

10 sts = 4″.

BODICE:

I hook. With Black make 5″ chain, work 2 rows in sc and change to Navy. Work 1 sc row and change to Teal. Work 1 row sc and change to Dark Red for 1 row. Now 1 row of Teal, 1 row of Navy and at the end of this row make 22 chs. Sc back in Black, change to Dark Red, work 2 rows same as length of Black, on third row add 3 chs, sc back into 3rd ch and sc across row. Work 1 more row in Dark Red, switch to Black for one row, Navy for 1 row, switch to Teal and work across row leaving last 3 sts unworked. Work 1 more row of Teal, 1 row Navy, 1 row Black, 1 row Dark Red, 1 row Black, 1 row Navy, 2 rows Teal. Ch 1 with Navy, now sc into Teal across row. Work 1 row Black including ch 1 at end of row. Switch to Dark Red and work 1 row even. On second row work across row leaving last 2 sts unworked. Work 2 more rows in Dark Red, 1 row in Black, change to Navy and work 15 sts (counting first ch 1 st), work 1 row Teal, 1 row Dark Red, 1 row Teal, 1 row Navy, 4 rows Black, 1 row Navy, 1 row Teal, 1 row Dark Red, 1 row Teal, 1 row Navy, change to Black and work sc across row and work 21 chs. Work back in Dark Red and work 2 more rows of Dark Red, on next row add 2 chs, work back 1 row of Black, 1 row of Navy. Next row (neck edge) count down to 10th st and attach Teal, work 1 row, attach Dark Red and work leaving last 2 sts undone. Next row attach Teal 2nd st down from neck, on next row attach Navy and work 1 row, next row Black and repeat striping to match other front panel.

SKIRT:

Work in dc. With Black pick up at beginning of left front panel and place a marker on each side seam. Inc 1 st every other row at marker and work striping as follows: 4 rows Black, 1 row Teal, 1 row Dark Red, 1 row Teal, 13 rows Navy, 1 row Teal, 1 row Dark Red, 1 row Teal, 4 rows Black, 2 rows Teal, 3 Dark Red, 2 Teal, and end with 6 Black.

Ruffle border: With Black work 2 tc in each st for 1 row and work 1 row of 1 tc in each st. Break off.

SLEEVES:

Make two. Ch 20 in Black, dc back into 4th ch from hook and work dc to end, connect to form circle with sl st into top ch of ch 3, ch 3 and work in the round 5 rows in Black (on 3rd row inc 1 st at beg of row) and every other row until armhole dec. Work colors as follows: 2 rows Teal, 3 Dark Red, 2 Teal, 4 Black, 1 Teal, 1 Dark Red, 1 Teal, and with Navy attach yarn on 5th st from ch 3 center (armhole), ch 3, work dc until center of row, work inc (2 sts in same sp) leaving last 4 sts before ch 3 center unworked. Next row dec 1 st at each end and inc at center. Continue working straight with dec at arm edge but inc at center every row for 8 rows. Break off.

Cuff: With Black work 2 tc in each st attach to other end with sl st. Break off. To set in sleeve, sew shoulder seams, gather top of shoulder of sleeve. Work 1 row of sc around bodice armhole. Set sleeve in, centering gathers at shoulder.

Border in Navy: On left side of work, in sc, work 4 rows. Break off. On right side, work 2 rows in sc, on 3rd row work buttonholes by chaining and skipping over sc from previous row, making hole large enough for button to fit through. Work 4 scs and work buttonhole. Continue in this manner making as many buttonholes as desired. Sc back and sc arnd neck, ch 3, work 1 row of dc, ch 4, turn, work 1 row in tc working 2 tc sts in each st, ch 4, turn, work 1 tc in each st. Break off.
Gather 1 yd. of lace (optional) to measure inside of collar and sew down.
Weave velvet ribbon through dc row at neck.
Gather the rest of lace to fit at bottom border and sew in.

POCKETS:

Make two. With G hook and Dusty Pink ch 7. Sc and work inc at each end until 20 sts, work even for 4″ from beginning. Work 1 row dc and on next row work 2 dc in each st. Break off.

DIAMONDS:

Ch 3, work sc into first ch, ch 2, turn, work sc in same space (inc). Work 2 sc in next space (inc), ch 2, turn, work inc at each end (6 sts on this row) repeat inc at either end until 10 sts on row, turn, sl st 1 ch 2, work 7 sts across row, turn, sl st 1, work

120

5 sts across row, turn, cont to dec in same manner until 2 sts remain. Break off. Border in sc in contrasting color.
Make 9 Aqua with Royal Blue trim.

ROUNDS:

Ch 4, join with sl st ch 2, work 7 sc, join with sl st, ch 2 work 2 sts in each sp, join with sl st. Break off. Border with contrasting color in sc.
Make eight Aqua with Royal Blue trim.
Make nine Dusty Pink with Hot Pink trim.

VELVET PANEL DOWN BACK OF COAT:

With Hot Pink, ch 7, work sc into 3rd ch from hook, work sc back and forth until piece measures 16″. Dec 1 st each end every other row until 2 sts remain. Break off. Border in Dusty Pink.

TWO ROUNDS WITH TAILS:

Work in Aqua trimmed with Royal Blue. Make round same as other rounds, but add one more row of sc, join row with sl st and work ch 2 and 5 sc across next 5 sts. Work back and forth in this manner for 4″. Border in Royal Blue.

EPAULETS:

Work with double-weight worsted wool and trim in velvet.
Ch 7, work 5 sc across row. Work back and forth in sc for 8½″. Dec 1 st each end every other row until 2 sts remain. Break off and border in velvet. Cut felt to fit panel and sew in place. Sew onto shoulder working 1 Dark Red panel in center and 2 Navy panels on either side. Sew down to side of sleeve bringing points together and leaving slight bulge.
Refer to color photos for placement of diamonds, rounds, and other design elements.

Victorian Bed Jacket

Materials:

1 lb. 4 oz. Plum ribbon, ⅛"–¼" thick.
2 yds. Beige ribbon, for trimming flowers (if desired).

Hook:

Size H aluminum.

With Plum ribbon ch 48. Work from top down.

Row 1: Dc into 4th ch from hook, work * 2 dc into next st (inc) 1 dc into each of next 2 sts, repeat from * ending with ch 3, turn.

Row 2: Work * 2 dc, ch 1, 2 dc in the middle of inc st from row below, work 1 dc into next 3 spaces. Repeat from * ending with ch 3, turn.

Row 3: Repeat Row 2 (you will always have 1 extra dc between incs every row). Cont for 22 rows. Divide work as shown in diagram. Ch 3 and work until joining. At that point work inc and cont around back of work leaving 3 panels undone for sleeves, work around the other side to the other front, ch 3, turn (sleeves will be worked separately later). Continue working around for body of jacket for 9 rows, sc around sides and neck of jacket. Pick up around sleeve and work 4 rows in pattern on each sleeve.

BORDER:

With Beige, attach ribbon to center of shell st on the bottom border.

Row 1: Ch 3, dc, ch 1, 2 dc in same space, skip 2 sts in 3rd space * dc, ch 1, dc, skip 2 sts in 3rd space work 2 dc, ch 1, 2 dc, skip 2 and repeat from *.

Row 2: Reverse shell pattern working 1 dc, ch 1, 1 dc, in 2 dc shell and vice versa.

Row 3: Repeat Row 1.

Row 4: Sl st to center of shell (ch 1 sp) ch 1, dc into next shell sp, ch 3, sl st back into top of dc (picot made) * ch 1, dc, picot work 2 more dc with picot ending with ch 1 sc into next shell ch 1 sp and repeat from *.

Sleeve border: With Beige, attach yarn to underarm. * Sc in next 2 sts, p in next st. Repeat from * arnd. Repeat for second sleeve.

attach sleeve here

Victorian Underwear

Sizes:

Instructions are for sizes 6 to 8.
Jacket: up to 34″ bust.
Pants: One size fits all.

Materials:

Rayon chenille, 20 1-oz. skeins.
12 Buttons.
4 Lined 4″ stays (optional).
Elastic thread.

Hook:

Size H aluminum, or size to obtain gauge.

Gauge:

4 dc = 1″.

x = inc

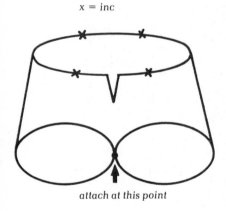

attach at this point

Pants

Make a chain to measure hip size and work 1 row dc on ch. Work 2 more rows of dc and join with sl st to form circle (work will be done in the round from now on). On 4th row, ch 3, work dc until middle of left front, work 2 sts in same space (inc) and work around to other marker points shown in diagram and inc at each point. Cont repeating 4th row until 16 rows from start are completed. Divide work in half from center point down from waist opening and center point of back. Tie these 2 sts tog and work one leg at a time (see diagram). Work around until desired length and on last row dec by skipping over every other st. Work other leg to correspond.

WAISTBAND:

Make a ch 6″ long and work 1 row of sc. Next sc picking up only the back of the st. Repeat this row working back and forth until piece measures comfortably around waist. Join bottom of band to top of pants with elastic thread leaving opening in front. Sc around placket opening, work ch 3 and skip 1 sc for buttonholes. Sew buttons to correspond with buttonhole openings.

Make 2″ ch and work pattern same as waistband. Weave ends together and sew to bottom of pants with elastic thread horizontally to prevent stretching.

Vest

Make 48 chs.

BACK:

Work in pattern and inc 1 st each end on 3rd row and every other row until piece measures 7″ or 12 rows.

ARMHOLE:

Sl st to 5th st, ch 3, work across row leaving last 4 sts undone, turn, sl st to 5th st, ch 3 work across. Dec 1 st each side three times. Work even until 12 rows.

SHOULDER:

Sl st to 5th st. Ch 3, work across row to last 4 sts. Turn, sl st to 5th st, ch 3, work 3 dc. Break off. Work sts on other side to correspond.

FRONT:

Make two. Ch 24, work seam same as back but on 7th row start inc for bust. Work to 16th st, inc (3 dc in same space) work to end, turn and work 1 more inc in center dc of inc from previous row. Continue working side seam same as back without inc at bust until 12 rows. Work armhole same as back. At the same time, dec 1 st at neck edge every row until 12 rows, turn sl st to 4th st, ch 3, work 7 dc, ch 3 turn, work 3 dc. Break off.

Finishing: Work 1 row of sc around armholes and all around bottom, sides and neck of vest. Work 3 rows sc on left side and work 2 rows of sc on right side. On 3rd row make buttonholes same as on pants. Sew buttons to correspond. Sew stays to form V at an angle at points of jacket.

For next size up: Work 3 more rows of sc arnd each panel of vest before sewing side seams together.

Jacqueline Henderson

Jacqueline Henderson has designed crocheted garments for key magazines, fashionable New York boutiques and many celebrities. Her designs and patterns have appeared regularly over a period of eight years in Woman's Day as well as McCall's and American Home Crafts. The boutiques include D-D-Dominick, Serendipity, and Allen & Cole. Her work is owned and worn by Judy Collins, Grace Slick, and Yoko Ono. In addition she designed the costume worn by Gwen Verdon in her solo number in the Broadway hit musical "Chicago." Her work has also been featured in Viva, Ebony, and New York magazine. She has designed for Coats & Clark, and has been included in the books Creative Crochet and Crochet Fashions & Furnishings. Her work has been exhibited in Julie: Artisans' Gallery, BFM, and The 380 Galleries.

128

"*All the things I design are made in sections. This is more or less my trademark. I work things this way because it enables me to get more texture into the crochet, along with a greater variety of shapes and design combinations. Things designed this way, though, tend to require longer, wordier instructions. But just because a set of instructions is long doesn't necessarily mean that the project itself is more complicated. Sometimes I have a hard time convincing people that this is really so. For example, for as long as I've been working for magazines their editors have been presenting many of my designs as if they were for advanced crocheters only, when many are actually for average crocheters or even beginners. While some of the things I design can seem frightening to a novice, all that's normally required is knowing the basic stitches and being able to follow abbreviated instructions. My instructions demand the undivided attention of the person following them—not one eye on the television and one eye on the step-by-step. But there's a big difference between something that's difficult because it's hard to understand and something that requires more than the average amount of concentration. Some of my things do take a little longer to make than the average crochet project, and I am aware of the fact that some people do become frustrated when something can't be completed very quickly. This, however, is an attitutde that's often very frustrating to me as a designer. I think we're living in an age of what I like to call fast crafts—and I think that's unfortunate. I hope there are a lot of other people who think as I do, because they're the ones I'm really designing for.*"

Jacqueline Henderson

Pink Petal Pillow

Size:

Round, diameter 19″.

Materials:

Knitting worsted-weight yarn worked double strands throughout.

Pink	2 skeins (4 oz.)
Yellow-Green	1 skein (4 oz.)
Forest Green	3 skeins (4 oz.)

1 ¼ yds. 45″-wide Muslin.
2 lbs. Polyester fiber.

Hook:

Size H aluminum or size to obtain gauge.

Gauge:

3 sc = 1″.

SIDE ONE:

Petal: Make seven.
Round 1: Use Yellow-Green. Ch 24, begin in 4th ch st from hk, sc each st across, ch 2, turn.
Round 2: *Work back lps only.* Sc each st across to ch 3 sp, sl st in ch 3 sp. Fasten off. Do not turn. Use Pink. In ch 3 sp at break-off st, work sc, ch 2, sc, work sc across foundation ch omitting last 4 sts, ch 2, turn.
Round 3: *Work back lps only throughout.* Sc each st to ch 2 sp, in ch 2 sp work sc, ch 2 and sc, sc in next Pink sc, sk sl st, sc across next side omitting last 2 sts, ch 2, turn.
Round 4: Sc across to ch 2 sp, sc, ch 2, sc in ch 2 sp, sc across next side omitting last 4 sts, ch 2, turn.
Rounds 5 and 6: Rep Round 4.
Round 7: Sc across to ch 2 sp, sc, ch 2 and sc in ch 2 sp, sl st next st. Fasten off. This side is right side. Petal should measure 7½″ from tip to bottom and 3½″ at widest part.

Ground: (Worked on petal)

Row 1: Work loosely throughout. Use Forest Green. Right side facing you, begin in last sc made in Row 7 of petal. *Work back loops only.* Sc in next sl st, work 2 sc, ch 2 and 2 sc, *place marker in ch 2 sp*, sc each st to within turning ch at end tip of ridge, * in tip of ch 2 work sc, sk to next free sc on previous ridge work 3 dc, * sk 2 sts, rep from * to *, sc next ch st, ch 1 turn.

Row 2: *Work both lps.* [Sk 2 sts, in next st work 3 dc, ch 2 and 3 dc (shell), sk 2 sts, sc] 3 times; ch 1, turn.

Row 3: Sl st working back lps next 3 dc, sc in ch 2 sp [sk 3 dc, shell in sc (both lps), sk 3 dc, sc in ch 2 sp] twice, ch 1, turn.

Row 4: Sl st working back lps next 3 dc, sc in ch 2 sp, shell in next sc, sc in next ch 2 sp, ch 1, turn.

Row 5: Sl st working back lps next 3 dc, sc in ch 2 sp, shell in next sc, *place marker in ch 2 sp of shell* sk 3 sl sts, sc in ch 1, sc over side of next sc, sl st back lps next 3 dc, sc next ch 1, sc over side of next sc, skip ch 2, over side of sc work 2 hdc, ch 2, 2 hdc.

LEFT SIDE:

Row 1: Sk 3 foundation ch sts, in next foundation ch st work 3 dc, (sk to ch 2 tip of next ridge, sc, sk 2 sts, 3 dc next st) twice, sc in ch 2 tip of next ridge, ch 1, turn.

Row 2: (Sk 2 sts, shell in next st, sk 2 sts, sc next st) twice, ch 1, turn.

Row 3: Sl st working back lps next 3 dc, sc in ch 2 sp, shell in next sc, sc in ch 2 sp, ch 1, turn.

Row 4: Sl st next 3 dc, sc in ch 2 sp, shell in next sc, sk 3 sl st, sc in ch 1 sp, ch 1, turn.

Row 5: Sl st next 3 dc, sc in ch 2 sp, shell in next sc, *place marker in ch 2 sp of shell* sk 3 sl st, sc in ch 1 sp, sc over side of next sc, sl st next 3 dc, sc in ch 1 sp, sc over side of next sc. Continue sl st in back lps, work loosely across Pink to within ch 2 sp at tip, ch 1, sl st, in beginning Forest Green sc. *Place marker in last st made.* Piece should measure 8″ in length and 7½″ at widest part. Fasten off. Repeat on remaining 6 petals.

Joining: Take two pieces. Place right side of first piece against left side of second. Join sts between markers on wrong side with sc sts, working back lps only. Be sure to include ch 1 sts and sc sts on their sides as sts to be worked.

CENTER:

Row 1: Use Yellow-Green. Ch 7, join with sl st in beginning ch st to form ring. Ch 3 turn, 15 dc in ring, sl st top ch 3, ch 2 turn.

Row 2: *Work back lps only.* Hdc in sm sp as turning ch, 2 hdc in each st around, sl st in top of beginning ch 2. (32 sts counting ch 2) Turn.

Row 3: Work behind hdc row in free lps of previous row. 2 dc in each st around, sl st top beg dc. Fasten off.

Joining Center: Hold piece so that wrong side is facing you. Insert hdc ridge of yellow green center through center hole of piece (hdc ridge will be on right side of pillow). With Forest Green, whipstitch dc sts of Yellow-Green center to Forest Green sc on edge of hole.

SIDE TWO:

Repeat Side One.

INNER PILLOW:

Cut two pieces of muslin ¾″ larger all around than crochet pillow; sew ½″ seams leaving 6″ opening for stuffing. Turn inside out, stuff with polyester. Blind-stitch opening.

Finishing: Place wrong sides together. Using Forest Green, join edges halfway around with sl st in back lps only. Slide inner pillow in form, continue sl st to end. Fasten off.

Yellow Flower Pillow

Size:

18″ square.

Materials:

Knitting worsted-weight yarn worked double strands throughout.

Dark Teal Blue	4 skeins (4 oz.)
Yellow	1 skein (4 oz.)
Green	1 skein (4 oz.)
Light Teal Blue	1 skein (2 oz.)

1¼ yds. 45″-wide muslin.

2 lbs. Polyester stuffing.

Hook:

Size H aluminum or size to obtain gauge.

Gauge:

4 dc = 1″.
Hexagon measures 9¼″ at widest part.

HEXAGON A:

Green Flower: **Make three.**

Round 1: Use Yellow. Ch 6, sl st in beg ch st to form ring. Ch 3, 11 dc in ring, sl st top beg ch 3, ch 2.

Round 2: *Work back lps only.* Sc in sm sp as ch 2, 2 sc in each st around, sl st top of ch 2 (total 24 sts). Fasten off.

Round 3: Use Green. *Work back lps only.* Beginning in any st, work 1 sc in each of next 3 sts; * ch 9 (foundation chain), in 3rd ch st from hk work sc, hdc next st, dc next st, trc next st, dc next st, hdc next st, sc next st (petal formed); ** sc in each of next 4 sts on circle; rep from * four times; rep from * to ** once; sc next sc on circle, sl st beg sc. Fasten off. Turn.

Round 4: Using Green, begin in any ch sp at tip of petal. * In ch 2 sp work sc, ch 2 and sc, sc in each of next 2 foundation ch sts, 2 trc in each of next 2 sts, sc in each of next 2 sts, sk last ch st on petal and next sc on circle, sc in each of next 2 sts, sk next 2 sts, *working back lps only* sc in each of next 2 sts, 2 trc in each of next 2 sts, sc in each of next 2 sts, rep from * sl st beg sc. Fasten off. Turn.

Round 5: (Note: Side facing you is right side.) Use Light Teal. Begin in first sc *after* ch 2 sp at tip of petal. * *Working back lps only*, sc in each of next 8 sts, sk last sc on petal, *working both lps* work next 2 sc as one (pull through lp on first st, pull through lp on next st, yo pull through all 3 lps on hk), sk first sc on next petal, *working back lps only* sc in each of next 8 sts, ch 2, sk ch 2 sp, rep from * five times, sl st in beg sc. Fasten off.

Round 6: Use Dark Teal. Beg in any ch 2 sp at tip of petal. * Work sc, ch 2 and sc in ch 2 sp, sc in each of next 2 sts, dc in each of next 3 sts, yo twice pull through lp on next st, sk 5 sts, pull through lp on next st, yo pull through 3 lps on hk, (yo pull through 2 lps) twice, dc in each of next 3 sts, sc in each of next 2 sts; rep from * five times, sl st beg sc, ch 2.

Round 7: *Work back lps only*. Ch 2, * sc, ch 2 and sc in ch 2 sp, sc in each st across to next ch 2 sp, rep from * around ending sl st in beg ch 2. Fasten off.

HEXAGON B:

Yellow Flower: **Make two.**

Repeat Hexagon A substituting Green for Rounds 1 and 2, and Yellow for Rounds 3 and 4.

HEXAGON C:

Blue Flower: **Make four.**

Repeat Hexagon A using Dark Teal for all rounds.

Joining Hexagons: Working back lps only, sc hexagons together on wrong side (use Dark Teal); see Diagram 1 for placement.

AREA E:

Have right side facing you. See Diagram 1. Start at either point marked E. Use Dark Teal.

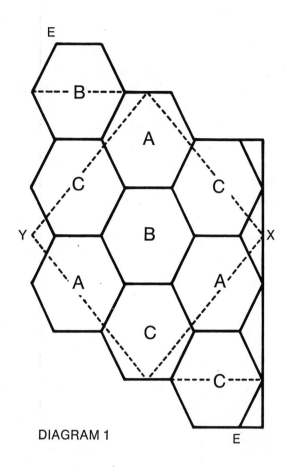

DIAGRAM 1

Section 1: *Working back lps only*, begin in sc *after* ch 2 corner.

Row 1: Trc next 2 sts, work trc in each of next 2 sts holding back last lps on hook, yo pull through all 3 lps (2 trc cluster made), dc next 3 sts, work dc in each of next 3 sts holding back last lps on hook, yo pull through all 4 lps on hook (3 dc cluster), hdc next 3 sts, sc next 2 sts, ch 1, turn.

Row 2: *Work front lps only.* Work 2 sc as one over next 2 sts as follows: Work sc to point where 2 lps are on hk, pull lp through next st, yo pull through all 3 lps on hk, hdc next 2 sts, dc next 4 sts, trc next 3 sts, ch 1 turn.

Row 3: *Work back lps only.* Sc next 5 sts, sl st next 5 sts, 2 sc in ch 2 sp at tip of hexagon.

Section 2:

Row 1: * Work *back lps only.* Sc next 2 sts, hdc next 3 sts, 3 dc cluster over next 3 sts, dc next 3 sts, 2 trc cluster over next 2 sts, trc next 2 sts, * yo twice, insert hook in ch 2 sp of hexagon corner, pull through lp, sk seam, pull lp through ch 2 sp of next hexagon, yo pull through 3 lps, (yo pull through 2 lps) twice, rep Row 1 of Section 1.

Row 3: *Work front lps only.* Rep Row 2 of Section 1, dtrc in next st, trc next 3 sts, ** dc next 4 sts, hdc next 2 sts, work 2 sc as one over next 2 sts, sl st next st, turn. **

Row 4: *Work back lps only,* sl st next 4 sts, sc next 6 sts, sk dtrc, sc next 6 sts, sl st next 5 sts, 2 sc in ch 2 sp at tip of hexagon.

Section 3: Rep Section 2.

Section 4:

Row 1: Rep Row 1 of Section 2 from * to *, ch 4, turn.

Row 2: *Work front lps.* Trc next 2 sts, rep Row 2 of Section 2 from ** to **.

Row 3: Sl st next 4 sts, sc next 6. Fasten off. Rep for opposite side (see Diagram 1).

Final Joining: Hold piece in position of Diagram 1. Place markers on points X and Y. Turn piece to wrong side. Piece will be in reverse of Diagram 1 (mirror image). Fold along dotted lines of Diagram 1. Pin edges to hold in place. Turn piece over. See Diagram 2 (pillow back). Using Dark Teal first single crochet together irregular edges.

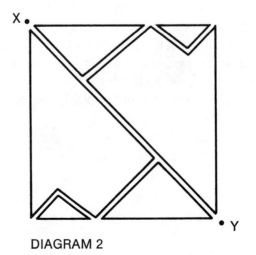

DIAGRAM 2

Note: To get a square be sure markers are at diagonal ends (see Diagram 2) when preparing final closing. Use a zipper along diagonal if you want cover to be removable.

INNER PILLOW:

Form by cutting two pieces of muslin ¾″ larger all around than piece; sew ½″ seams on 3 sides; turn and stuff; blind-stitch last side, slide pillow in crochet form, sl st diagonal closed (on right side) if not using zipper.

Jacket

Sizes:

Directions are for Medium size (12 to 14). Small (8 to 10) and Large sizes (16 to 18) are in parentheses. Jacket measures 21″ (19″, 23″) in width across back at underarm for a loose fit, 10½″ (9½″, 11½″) in width across each front piece at under arm, 29″ (28″, 30″) in length from back of neck to lower edge, 21″ (20½″, 21½″) in length at side seam, and 9″ (8″, 10″) in width across sleeve at upper arm.

Materials:

Bulky- or rug yarn-weight wool worked together with mohair throughout (100 percent wool, 2-oz. skeins).

Bulky	*Skeins*
Cherry Heather (A)	3
Camel (B)	2
Pale Straw Green Heather (C)	5
Curry Heather (D)	2
Chocolate Brown Heather (E)	3
Cafe au Lait Heather (F)	3
Loden Green Heather (G)	3
Light Chocolate Brown Heather (H)	3
Gray Heather (I)	3
Bright Brick Red (J)	2
Beige (K)	3

Mohair	*Skeins*
Strawberry	2
Dusty Rose	2
Celery Green	3
Pale Taupe	1
Pale Gray-Green	3
Dark Taupe	1

Pale Gray-Green	2
Medium Chocolate	2
Pale Lavendar	2
Raspberry	2
Light Pink	2

Hook:

Size H aluminum or size to obtain gauge.

Gauge:

4 sc with ch 1 sps between = 2″, 2 rows = 1″.

Back Body:

See Diagram 1.

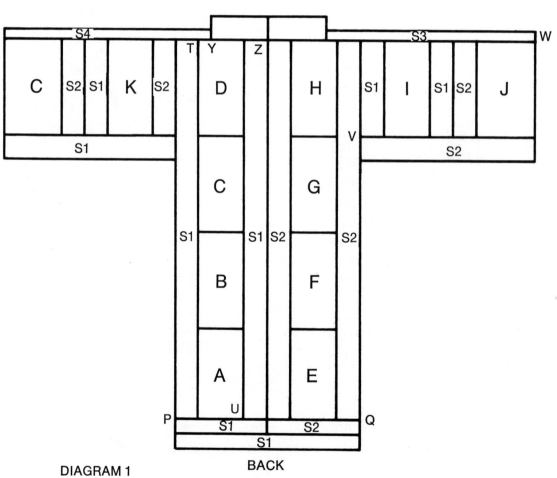

DIAGRAM 1

S = Stripe Band

BACK

FIRST STRIP:

(Consists of 4 color blocks and 2 bands of stripes).

Color Block A:
Row 1: Using color A, ch 30 [28, 32], sc in 4th ch st from hook, ch 1, * sk 1 st, sc, ch 1, rep from * across ending ch 2, turn.
Row 2: * Sk sc, sc in next ch 1 sp, ch 1, rep from * across, ending sc in turning ch 2 sp, ch 2, turn. (Should measure 8″ [7½″, 8½″] across). Rep Row 2 for pattern. Work in pattern until you have 20 rows. (Should measure approximately 7″ in height.) Fasten off.

Color Block B: Attach color B, work 20 rows (19, 21) in pattern. Fasten off.

Color Block C: Attach color C, work 20 rows (19, 21) in pattern. Fasten off.

Color Block D: Attach color D, work 20 rows (19, 21) in pattern. Fasten off.

Left Stripe Band 1: (See Diagram 1 for placement. Begin at T on diagram.)
Row 1: Work on side edge of Color Block strip from top to bottom. Use color E. Work sc over each end-of-row st. Mark this side as right side. Fasten off. Turn.
Row 2: Use color F. Begin in last st of Row 1. *Working front lps only* sc each st across. Fasten off. Do not turn.
Row 3: Use color G. Begin in first st of Row 2. *Working front lps only*, sc each st across. Fasten off. Do not turn.
Row 4: Use color I. Begin in first st of Row 3. *Working front lps only* sc each st across. Fasten off. Turn.

Right Stripe Band 1: Right side facing you, work right side edge of Color Block strip from bottom to top. (Begin at U on Diagram 1.) Rep Rows 1 through 4 of Left Stripe Band 1.

SECOND STRIP:

Color Blocks E through H: Work same as for First Strip, substituting color E for A, color F for B, color G for C and color H for D.

Left Stripe Band 2: (See Diagram 1 for placement.) Rep Stripe Band 1 from Row 1, substituting color A for E in Row 1, color K for F in Row 2, and color C for G in Row 3.

Row 4: Turn to right side, using color H, sc across in *back lps only*. Fasten off.

Right Stripe Band 2: With right side facing you, work from bottom to top same as for Left Stripe Band 2.

Joining Strips: Place two strips right sides together. Sc tog on wrong side with color H, working front and back lps only.

Bottom Stripe Band: (See Diagram 1.) With right side facing you, work as for Stripe Band 1 across length of bottom.

Row 5: Use color I. With right side facing you *working back lps only* sc around Bottom Stripe Band beginning at P on diagram and ending at Q.

Back Sleeves:

Work 4 blocks as for Color Block A [19 rows for 8 to 10] one each in colors I, J, K, and C.

RIGHT SLEEVE:

Color Block I: Count last row as top of the block. Working top to bottom on left side of block rep Rows 1 through 4 of left Stripe Band 1. Working bottom to top on right side of block rep Rows 1 through 4 of left Stripe Band 1.

Color Block J: Working top to bottom rep Left Stripe Band 2.

Joining: (See Diagram 1 for placement) Place Block I and Block J right sides tog, Left Stripe Band of J to Right Stripe Band of I. Sc tog wrong side with color H, working front and back lps only.

Underarm Stripe Band: Hold piece right side facing you so that I is on the right. Work across top using color A. Begin at V on diagram.

Row 1: Work sc across skipping every 4th st on the blocks and working 1 sc in each stripe of band. Work Rows 2 through 4 same as for Stripe Band 2.

Joining Right Sleeve to Body: (See Diagram 1 for placement.) With right sides tog, Stripe Band 1 of I to Stripe Band 2 of body, sc tog on wrong side with color H working front and back lps only.

Right Shoulder Stripe: ** (S3 on Diagram 1.) Hold piece (right side facing you) so that J is on the right. Use color E. Begin at W on diagram. Rep Row 1 of Underarm Stripe Band across sleeve work. Work sc in each stripe of band on body ** and sc in each of next 9 sts [7, 11] (sc and ch 1 sps) on block H. Fasten off.

LEFT SLEEVE:

Color Block K: Work top to bottom on left side of block. Work as for Left Stripe Band 1, Rows 1 through 4. Work from bottom to top on right side of block. Work as for Stripe Band 2.

Color Block C2: Working from bottom to top on right side of block work as for Stripe Band 2. Join C to K right sides tog. (See Diagram 1 for placement.) Stripe Band 2 of C to Stripe Band 1 of K, sc tog on wrong side with color H working front and back lps only.

Underarm Stripe Band: Hold piece (right side facing you) so that C2 is on your right. Work across top using color E. Begin at X on Diagram 1. Rep Row 1 of right sleeve Underarm Stripe Band. Work Rows 2 through 4 as for Stripe Band 1.

Joining Left Sleeve to Body: (See Diagram 1 for placement.) With right sides tog Stripe Band 2 of K to Stripe Band 1 of body, sc tog as for right sleeve.

Left Shoulder Stripe: (S4 on Diagram 1.) Hold piece (right side facing you) so that C2 is on your left. Begin at D. Count 9 [7, 11] sts to the right of Left Stripe Band 1 (Y on Diagram 1). With color A sc in each of 9 sts on D, sc in each stripe of bands on body. Over sleeve work sc in each stripe of bands and sc across blocks, skipping every 4th st. Fasten off.

Front Body:

See Diagram 2, page 146.

FIRST STRIP:

Color Blocks: Work same as for first stripe on back to Block D.

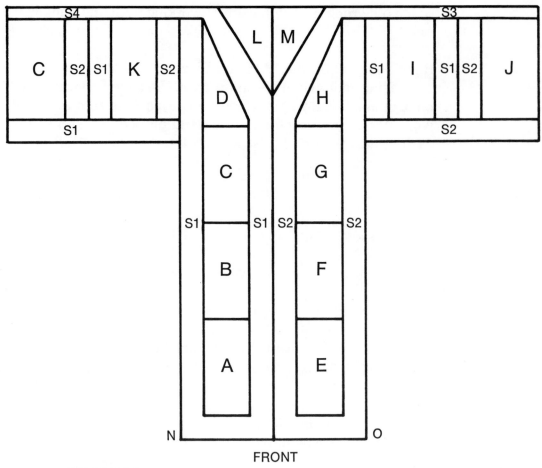

FRONT

DIAGRAM 2

Color Block D:
Row 1: Work in pattern.
Row 2: Work even, ch 2, turn.
Row 3: Sk 1 ch sp, sk next sc, sc next ch 1 sp, (dec) work in pattern across, ch 2, turn. Rep Rows 2 and 3 alternately until you have 20 rows (19, 21). Fasten off.

Stripe Bands: Hold strip so that dec edge is on the side at the right. Work even edge beginning at shoulder end, repeat as for Stripe Band 1.

SECOND STRIP:

Color Blocks: Work same as for back second strip to color block H.

Color Block H: Work same as for front Color Block D in front first strip.

146

Stripe Bands: Hold strip to that dec edge is on the side at left. Work even edge beginning at bottom end, rep as for Stripe Band 2.

Front Sleeves:

Work same as for back. Join sleeves to body same as for back.

SHOULDER STRIPES:

Right Shoulder Stripe: Rep as for back from **to **.

Left Shoulder Stripe: (S4 on Diagram 2). Hold piece (right side facing you) so that C2 is on your left. Begin at D. With color A sc in each stripe of bands on body, over sleeve work sc in each stripe of bands and sc across blocks, skipping every 4th st. Fasten off.

Final Joining: Join front sections to back with sc sts on wrong side, working back lps only.

FRONT OPENING STRIPE BANDS:

Left Front: Beg at N in Diagram 2. Rep as for Stripe Band 1, working 3 sc in each of 2 corner sts and dec 2 at shoulder seams; end at Z on Diagram 1.

Right Front: Beg at Z on Diagram 1. Rep as for Stripe Band 2, dec 2 at shoulder seams and working 3 sc in corner sts; end at O on Diagram 2.

Neck Section:

Area L (see Diagram 2): Use color D.
Row 1: Begin at Z on Diagram 1 in first st left of seam, (sc, sk 1, sc next st) across to shoulder seam, work sts before and after seam as one (dec), rep ( ) to corner shell, (3 sc sts) ch 2 turn.
Row 2: Sk next ch sp and next sc, sc next ch sp (dec), work ch 1, sk next sc, sc in ch sp (pattern st) to within shoulder seam, work dec as follows: Insert hk in next ch sp, pull through lp, sk sc st, insert hk in next ch sp, pull through lp, yo, pull through all 4 lps on hk, work in pattern st to end, ch 2, turn. Rep Row 2 until fill-in is even-edged triangle. Fasten off. Rep for Area M (see Diagram 2) with color H.

Zipper: Use 16″ medium-weight separating zipper. Sew in leaving blocks A and E free.

Butterfly Shawl

Size:

98″ wide × 50″ long, including 14″ fringe.

Materials:

4-ply knitting worsted:

Bright Olive (A)	2 skeins (4 oz. each)
Lime (B)	1 skein
Dark Rust (C)	1 skein
Bright Pink (D)	1 skein
Sky Blue (E)	1 skein
Light Rust (F)	1 skein
Lavender (G)	1 skein
Cream Yellow (H)	8 skeins

Hook:

Size E aluminum or size to obtain gauge.

Gauge:

3 dc = ¾″, 1 dc row = ¾″.

Note: Following are abbreviations for stitches used in this piece:
dtrc—double treble crochet (yo 3 times)
tr trc—triple treble crocket (yo 4 times)
quint dc—quintuple double crochet (yo 5 times)
sixtuple dc—sixtuple double crochet (yo 6 times)

Butterfly—Section A:

BUTTERFLY:

Make half a butterfly consisting of top wing, bottom wing, and body. (See Diagram 1, page 150.)

Top Wing:
Row 1: With A, form a 3 lp foundation chain as follows: (ch 4, dc in 4th ch from hk) three times. Do not turn. Working along dc edge of lps, * sc over side of dc; ch 10, starting in 3rd ch st

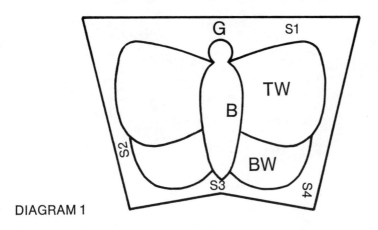

DIAGRAM 1

S = side
TW = top wing
BW = bottom wing
B = body
G = Ground

from hk, work sc in each of next two ch sts, dc next 2 sts, trc next 2 sts and dc next 2 sts; sc over same foundation dc; rep from * in each of next 2 lps (3 petals formed). Fasten off. (Each petal should measure about 2″ from dc base to tip. Foundation should measure about 2½″ across.)

Row 2: With B, turn piece to other side; sl st in last sc of Row 1, * sc in each of next 8 sts up petal, work sc, ch 3, and sc in ch 2 sp at tip of petal, sc in each of next 8 sts down foundation chain of petal **, sk next 2 sc, rep from * once; rep from * to **, sl st in next sc, turn.

Row 3: Sc in each of next 9 sc, *in ch 3 sp, work sc, ch 3, and sc **, sc in each of next 5 sc, skip the rem 4 sc on this petal and 4 sc on next petal. Work 5 sc, rep from * once; rep from * to **, *mark this ch 3 sp with safety pin*, sc in each of the next 9 sc, (ch 3, sc in ch 3 sp of foundation lp) three times; ch 3, sl st in beg sc. Fasten off. Turn.

Row 4: With A, beg in marked ch 3 sp; *work sc, ch 3, and sc in ch 3 sp **, sc in each of next 3 sts, sk 2 sts, dc next 2 sts, sk 2 sts, sc next 3 sts, rep from *once; rep from *to **. Fasten off. Turn.

Row 5: With B, beg in last ch 3 sp of Row 4, * work 3 sc in ch 3 sp **, sk 4 sc, work 4 trc in each of next 2 dc, sk 4 sc, rep from * once; rep from * to **. Fasten off. Turn. (Piece should measure about 3½ ″ from foundation to top of this row.)

Row 6: With A; beg in last sc worked on Row 5, work 2 sc in first sc, * ch 10, starting in 3rd ch st from hk, work 2 sc, 2 dc, 2 trc, 2 dc, in the 8 ch sts (petal formed); sk 4 sts, sc in each of next 2 sts, rep from * three times. Fasten off. Turn.

Row 7: With B beg in last sc worked on Row 6, work sl st, sk next sc, * sc in each of next 8 sts up petal, work sc, ch 3, and sc in ch 2 sp at tip of petal, sc in each of next 8 sts down foundation chain of petal **, sk 2 sc sts, rep from * twice; rep from * to **, sk next sc, sl st next sc, turn.

Row 8: Sc in each of next 9 sc, *in ch 3 sp work sc, ch 3, and sc **, work sc in each of next 5 sts, sk 4 sc rem on this petal and 4 sc on next petal, work sc in each of next 5 sts, rep from * twice; rep from * to **, *mark this ch 3 sp with safety pin*, sc in each of next 9 sts. Fasten off. Turn.

Row 9: With C beg in marked sp, * work sc, ch 3, and sc **, sc in each of next 3 sts, sk 2 sts, dc in each of next 2 sts, sk 2 sts, sc in each of next 3 sts, rep from * twice; rep from * to **. Fasten off. Turn.

Row 10: With Color D beg in last ch 3 sp of Row 9, * work sc, ch 3, and sc **, ch 2, in each of 2 dc between petals wk 2 trc holding back last lp of each trc on hk, yo pull through all 5 lps on hk, ch 2 rep from * twice; rep from * to **. Fasten off. Turn.

Row 11: With A beg in last ch 8 sp of Row 10, work 3 sc in each ch sp across, (a total of 30 sts). Ch 4, turn.

Row 12: Work 3 dc in first sc, (sk 3 sts, sc next sc, sk 3 sts, in next st work shell of 3 dc, ch 3 and 3 dc) twice, sk 3 sc, sl st next st, turn.

Row 13: Sc in each of next 3 dc (sc in ch 3 sp, sk 3 dc, work shell in sc, sk 3 dc,) twice, sc in top of ch 4, turn.

Row 14: Work 3 dc in sc, sk 3 dc, sc in ch 3 sp, sk 3 dc, work shell in sc, sk 3 dc, sl st in ch 3 sp, turn.

Row 15: Sc in next 3 dc, sc in ch 3 sp, sk 3 dc, shell in sc, sk 3 dc, sc in top of ch 4. Fasten off. Turn.

Row 16: With C, work edging on four sides of wing. First Edge (side edge): Beg in last sc of Row 15. Sc, sk dc, work shell of (3 dc, ch 3, and 3 dc in next dc), sk 1 dc, sc in ch 3 sp, p, (picot-worked ch 3, sc in 3rd ch st from hk,) (sc next 7 sts. Be careful not to work in sl sts or ch sps; work p) three times; sc in each of next 2 sts, p, sc sm sp. (5 p sts on edge). Second Edge (seam edge): Sc in each of next 2 end-of-row sc, sc in next 10 sts on petal, sc in each of next 3 end-of-row sts, sc in next 10 sts on petal (Total–26 sts from p). *Mark this edge with safety pin.* Third Edge (body edge): Ch 3, 4 sc over each of next four ch 3 sps. Fourth Edge (top edge): Ch 3, 2 sc in next sc, *mark this ch 3 sp with thread.* Sc in next 5 sts, p, sc next 4 sc on petal, work sc over next 3 end-of-row sc, p, sc next 7 sts, p, sc 3 sts on petal, sc over next 3 end-of-row sc, sc in ch 4 sp, p, sc sm sp, 2 sc in next ch 4 sp, sl st beg sc. (4 p sts on edge). Fasten off. (Wing should measure approximately 9½" at top edge and 7½" side edge.)

Bottom Wing:

Row 1: With E, ch 6, join with sl st to form ring, ch 3, 7 dc in ring, ch 3, turn. (Ch 3 counts as dc).

Row 2: Dc sm sp as turning ch, 2 dc in each dc st around, end 1 dc in top st of turning ch, (total 15 sts). Ch 3, turn.

Row 3: Dc sm sp as turning ch, dc next stitch. *2 dc next st, dc next st, rep from * across omitting turning ch, (total 21 sts). Fasten off. Turn. (Straight edge of half-circle just formed should measure approximately 3½".)

Row 4: With A, beg in last dc worked on Row 3, work 2 sc, * ch 6, sc in 3rd ch from hk, sc next st, dc next st, trc last ch st, (triangle formed). Sk 3 sts, 2 sc in next st, rep from * four times. Fasten off. Turn.

Row 5: With B, beg in last sc worked on Row 4, work 3 dc, sk next sc and 4 sts of triangle, * in ch 2 sp at tip of triangle work sc, ch 3, and sc **; in first sc between triangles work 3 dc, ch 3, work 3 dc in second sc, rep from * three times, rep from * to **, *mark this ch 8 sp with safety pin*, sk 1 sc, work 3 dc in end sc. Fasten off. Turn.

Row 6: With D, beg in marked sp, work sc, ch 3, and sc, (ch 2, work sc, ch 3, and sc in next ch 3 sp) eight times. Fasten off. Turn.

Row 7: With A, beg in first dc worked on Row 5, work dc in each of 3 dc, ch 3, (sk sc, ch 3, sc), work 3 sc over ch 2 sp, ch 3, 4 dc over next ch 2 sp, 5 trc over next ch 2 sp, p, 5 trc over next ch 2 sp, (ch 3, 3 sc over next ch 2 sp) four times, ch 3, work dc in each of the 3 end sts of row 5. Fasten off. Turn.

Row 8: With C, *work edging*: Beg in last dc worked on Row 7, (work sc in each of next 3 sts, 4 sc over ch 3 sp, p) five times. *Mark with thread first p made.* Sc in each of next 5 trc, in p work 2 dc, p, and 2 dc, sc in each of next 5 trc, p, sk 4 dc, (4 sc over next ch 3 sp, sc in each of next 3 sts, p) twice. Seam Edge: Working over sides of sts, 2 sc over each of next 2 dc, 2 sc over sc, 2 dc over each of next 3 sts, 2 trc in ch sp, 2 dc over each of next 3 sts, 2 sc over sc, 2 sc over each of next 2 dc, (total 26 sts), ch 3, sl st in beg sc. Fasten off. (9 p sts on edge). Seam edge should measure approximately 7".

Join seam edge to top wing edge marked with safety pin as follows: Place wings tog so that the top wing is on top with thread marker to your left and bottom is on bottom with thread marker on your left. Omitting corner ch 3 sps and ps, fit edges tog. Using darning needle join edges tog with overcast st, working *back* lps only.

Body:

Row 1: With F, hold wings so that edge with thread markers is on top and bottom wing is on your right. Ch 9, sc in p marked with thread, sc next 7 sc, sc in each of next 2 ch 3 sps, sc next 16 sc, sc in ch 3 sp marked with thread, ch 11, turn.

Row 2: Beg in 2nd ch st from hk, work 2 clusters as follows: (Over each of next 5 ch sts work dc holding back last lp of each dc on hk, yo, pull through all 6 lps on hk) twice, 2 sc in next sc, sc next 4 sts, (dc in each of next 2 sts holding back last lp of each dc on hk, yo, pull through 3 lps) four times, (trc in each of next 2 sts holding back last lp of each trc on hk, yo, pull through all 3 lps on hk) three times, dc in each of next 8 sc, dc in each of next 3 ch sts, sc next 6 ch sts. Fasten off.

Make second half of butterfly (top wing, bottom wing, and body). Fit body edges tog. Using darning needle join with overcast st, working *back* lps only.

Make two more butterflies.

BUTTERFLY GROUND:

Area G:

Round 1:

Side 1: With H, (see Diagram 1 for position.) Hold butterfly so that top wings are on top. Beg in tip of top wing at your right. In ch 3 sp at tip work (sc, ch 3 and sc), ch 3, sk 3 dc, sc next sc, ch 3, sk 2 sc, sc; * ch 3, sk p, sc, (ch 3, sk 2 sts, sc) twice ** rep from * across omitting last 3 sts on this edge, sk 2 sts, trc in next st, ch 5, sk 4 sts on body head, sc next st, ch 5, sc in center st on head, ch 5, sk next 5 sts on head, sc, ch 5, trc in first sc on left wing edging, sk 2 sts, sc, ch 3, sk 2 sts, sc, rep from * to ** omitting last 3 sts, sk 3 dc, in ch 3 sp at corner work sc, ch 3, and sc. (Total 32 ch sps).

Side 2: Ch 3, sk 3 dc, sc, rep from * to ** across to within last 2 ps on top wing, ch 3, sc in st after next p, ch 3, sk last p on top wing and first p on bottom wing (at seam) sc next st, (ch 3, sk 2 st, sc) twice, † rep from * to ** to corner omitting last 3 sts, sk sc and dc, dc in next dc, ch 5, dc sm sp, sk p; dc, ch 5 and dc in dc after p, sk dc and sc, sc next st. (Total 21 sps).

Side 3: Ch 3, sk 2 sts, sc, rep from * to ** to last p on this bottom wing, ch 3, sc in st after p, sk 5 sc, dc (last free sc on edge), sk 4 sts on body, sc next st; ch 3, sk 3 sts, sc in corner st; ch 3, sc next corner st; ch 3, sk 3 sts, sc in 4 sts, dc in first free st on bottom wing edging; sk 5 sts, sc; rep Side 2 from † (Total 27 ch sps).

Side 4: Ch 3, sk 2 sts; rep from * to ** to last p (at seam) on bottom wing, ch 3, sk this p and first p on top wing, sk next st, sc; (ch 3, sk 2 sts) twice; rep from * to ** to last p, ch 3, sk p, ch 3, sk 3 dc, sl st beg sc of side. (Total 19 ch sps).

Round 2:

Side 1: Sc, ch 3 and sc in ch 3 sp at tip, 3 sc in each of next 3 ch 3 sps, 3 dc in each of next 9 ch 3 sps, holding back last lp on hk work dc in next ch 3 sp, holding back last lp on hk work dc in ch 5 sp (on body), yo pull through all 3 lps on hk, work 5 sc in each of next 2 ch 5 sps holding back last lp on hk work dc in next ch 5 sp, holding back last lp on hk, work dc in next ch 3 sp on wing, yo pull through all 3 lps on hk, 3 dc in each of next 9 ch 3 sps 3 sc in each of next ch 3 sps, in corner ch 3 sp work sc, ch 3 and sc (total 86 sts across, between ch 3 sps).

Side 2: Work 3 sc in each of next 4 ch 3 sps, 3 dc in next 2 ch 3 sps, 3 trc in next 2 ch 3 sps, 3 dtrc in next 2 ch 3 sps, 3 trc in next ch 3 sp, 3 dc in next 2 ch 3 sps, 3 sc in next 2 ch 3 sps, 3 dc in next ch 3 sp, 3 trc in next ch 3 sp, 3 tr trc in next 2 ch 3 sps, 3 quit dc, (yo five times) in ch 5 sp, 4 sixtuple dc (yo six times) in same ch 5 sp, ch 12, sc same ch 5 sp (total 65 sts omitting ch 3 sp and ch 12).

Side 3: 3 Sc in next ch 5 sp, 3 dc in next ch 3 sp, 3 sc in next ch 3 sp, 2 dc in next 7 ch 3 sps, dtrc in next ch 3 sp, tr trc in next ch 3 sp, 3 sc in ch 3 sp at tip of body, tr trc in next ch 3 sp on wing, dtrc in next ch 3 sp, 2 dc in each of next 7 ch 3 sps, 3 sc in next ch 3 sp, 3 dc in next ch 3 sp, 3 sc in next ch 5 sp. (Total 53 sts omitting ch 12 sp at end of edge).

Side 4: Sc in next ch 5 sp, ch 12, 4 sixtuple dc in same ch 5 sp, 3 quint dc in same ch 5 sp, 3 tr trc in next 2 ch 3 sps, 3 trc in next ch 3 sp, 3 dc in next ch 3 sp, 3 sc in next 2 ch 3 sps, 3 dc in next 2 ch 3 sps, 3 trc in next ch 3 sp, 3 dtrc in next 2 ch 3 sps, 3 trc in next 2 ch 3 sps, 3 dc in next 2 ch 3 sps, 3 sc in each of next 4 ch 3 sps, sl st in beg sc of Side 1. *Mark this side with tag as right side!* Fasten off. (Total 64 sts omitting ch 3 sp and ch 12 sp at corners).

Row 3: With right side facing you, place butterfly so that Side 1 is on top. Beg at right corner sp, sk ch 3 sp, and next 19 sts, work sc next 3 sts, hdc next 3 sts, dc next 3 sts, trc next 3 sts, dtrc next 3 sts, tr trc next 6 sts, d trc next 6 sts, tr trc next 6 sts, dtrc next 3 sts, trc next 3 sts, dc next 3 sts, hdc next 3 sts, sc next 3 sts. Fasten off (total 48 sts).

Note: Side 1 should measure between corner ch 3 sps approximately 20½"; Sides 2, 3 and 4 from ch 3 corner sps to top of ch 8's approximately 15".

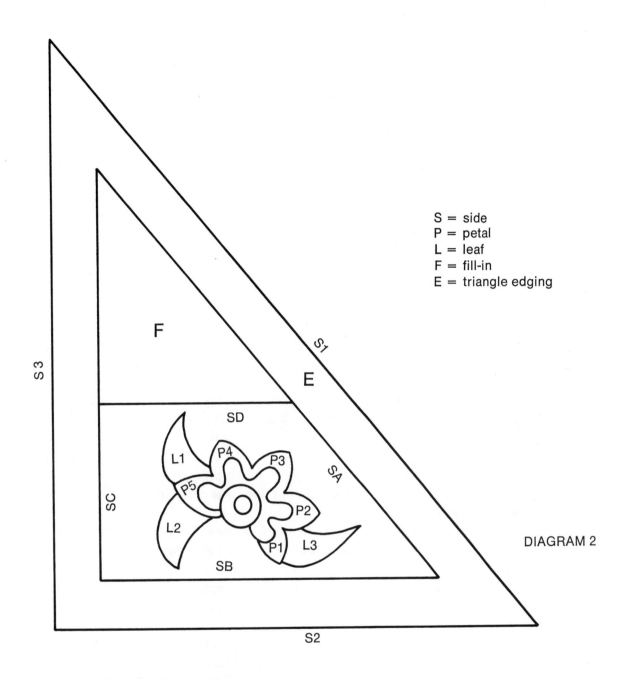

S = side
P = petal
L = leaf
F = fill-in
E = triangle edging

DIAGRAM 2

Flower Triangle—Section B:

FLOWER:

(See Diagram 2.)

Make seven.

Row 1: With F, ch 6, sl st first ch st to form ring, ch 3, work 13 dc in ring, sl st top of ch 3. Fasten off. Turn.

Row 2: With E, work 2 sc in each st around, sl st in beg sc (total 28 sts). Fasten off. *Turn piece to other side.*

Row 3: With G, beg in sl st; work sc, sc in next st, * ch 3, in next st work cluster as follows: holding back last lp of each dc on hk, work 4 dc, yo, pull through all 5 lps on hk; ch 3, sc in each of next 3 sts; rep from * four times, on 4th rep omit 3rd sc (7 unworked sts on circle edge). Fasten off. Turn.

Row 4: With E, beg in last st of Row 3; work sc, * over ch 3 sp work 3 hdc, in tip of cluster work 3 dc, p, and 3 dc, over ch 3 sp work 3 hdc, ** sk 1 sc, sl st next st, sk 1 sc; rep from * three times, rep from * to **; end sc in last sc. *Mark last petal made as petal* 5. Fasten off. *Do not turn.*

Row 5: With A, *First Leaf*—(beg in sl st between 4th and 5th petals). Work sc, ch 11; starting in 3rd ch st from hk work sc next 2 ch sts, dc next 3 sts, trc next 4 sts, sk 5 sts on petal 5, sl st next st. Turn.

Row 6: Sk sl st, work (p, sc in each of next 3 sts) three times, in ch 2 sp at tip work sc, p and sc, (sc in each of next 3 foundation ch sts, p) three times, sl st in beg sc (7 p sts on leaf). Fasten off. Turn. *Second Leaf*—working on same petal (5th petal) beg in 1st dc *after* p. Rep Rows 5 and 6 omitting ( ) at beg of Row 5. *Do not turn* after Row 6. *Third Leaf*—beg in sl st between 2nd and 1st petals. Rep Rows 5 and 6 omitting ( ) at beg of Row 5 and substituting petal 1 for petal 5. (See Diagram 3, page 159 to be sure your leaves are curving in the right direction.)

(See Diagram 3, page 159 to be sure your leaves are curving in the right direction.)

FLOWER OUTLINE:

Place flower B so that circle edge is on your left and leaves 1 and 2 are on top.

Side A: Beg in leaf 1 at tip p. Dc in sc after p, ch 3, sk 2 sts, dc ch 3; work trc, ch 3, trc and ch 3 in center st between next 2 ps, ch 3; dtrc in center st between next 2 ps; dtrc in center st between first 2 ps on leaf 2, ch 3; trc, ch 3 and dc in center st between next 2 ps, ch 3; sc in st before p at tip of leaf, ch 3; sc in st after p.

Side B: Ch 3, sk 2 sts, sc in st before next p, ch 3; trc in center st between next 2 ps; ch 3, dtrc in center st between next 2 ps, holding back last lp on hk; tr trc in first free st on circle edge, *holding back last lp on hk,* sk 2 sts on circle edge, dtrc in next st, *holding back last lp on hk* yo, pull through all 4 lps on hk (cluster made); ch 3, sk 2 sts on circle edge, in next st work tr trc, ch 3, and tr trc, ch 3; sc in dc before p at tip of petal, ch 3; hdc in center st between first 2 ps on leaf 3, ch 3; dc in center st between next 2 ps, ch 3; trc in 2nd sc after next p; ch 6, sc in 3rd ch st from hk, hdc next st, dc next st, trc next st, (triangle formed): sk 1 st on leaf dc next st.

Side C: Ch 3, sc in first st after p at tip of leaf, ch 3; sk 1 st, dc next st; trc in center st between next 2 ps, ch 3; dtrc in center st between next 2 ps, ch 3; sc in dc after p on petal, ch 3; dtrc in sl st between petals, ch 3; sc in dc before p on next petal, ch 3; ch 3; sc in dc before p on next petal, ch 3; sc in dc after p.

Side D; Ch 3, dtrc in sl st between petals, ch 3; in dc before p on next petal, ch 3; trc in dc after p on petal holding back last lp on hk; dtrc in center st between first 2 ps on Leaf 1, holding back last lp on hk, trc in center st between next 2 ps, holding back last lp on hk, yo, pull through all 4 lps on hk (cluster made), ch 3; sc in sc before p at tip of leaf, ch 3; sl st beg dc. *Do not break off.* (Side A should measure approximately 6¼"; Side B, 9½", Side C, 6½"; Side D, 5".)

Fill-In: (See Diagram 2.)

Row 1: Ch 1, turn, working over Side D, in ch 3 sp work sc, p and dc (p shell), over next ch 3 sp dc, ch 3 dc (V st), p shell in next st (top of cluster), V st in ch 3 sp, p shell in next ch 3 sp, sk next ch 3 sp, trc in sc, ch 3, turn.

Row 2: (Sk dc and p, V st in sc, p shell in ch 3 sp of V st) twice, V st in sc of next p shell, trc in turning ch 1, ch 1, turn.

Row 3: (P shell in ch 3 sp, V st in sc of p shell) twice, sk V st (dec) trc in top of turning ch 3, ch 3, turn.

Row 4: (P shell in ch 3 sp, V st in next sc) twice, trc in turning ch 1, ch 1, turn.

Row 5: P shell in ch 3 sp, V st in sc, p shell in ch 3 sp, sk p shell, trc in top of turning ch 3 (dec), ch 3, turn.

Row 6: V st in sc, p shell in ch 3 sp, V st in sc, trc in ch 1, ch 1, turn.

Row 7: P shell in ch 3 sp, V st in sc, sk V st, trc in top of turning ch 3 (dec), ch 3, turn.

Row 8: P shell in ch 3 sp, V st in sc, trc in ch 1, ch 1, turn.

Row 9: Work p shell in ch 3 sp, sk p shell, trc in top of turning ch 3 (dec), ch 3, turn.

Row 10: V st in sc, trc in ch 1. *Do not break off.* Mark edge with last trc made as Side 3; mark next edge Side 2, and longest edge as Side 1. (Side 1 should measure approximately 13½", Side 2, 8¾"; Side 3, 10½".)

Edging: (See Diagram 2.)

Row 11:

Side 1: Ch 3 turn, over ch 3 sp of last V st made work, 3 dc, ch 3 and 4 dc, ** counting trcs as ch sps * work p shell over next ch sp, V st next ch sp, rep from * across ** (total 9 p shells, 8 V sts), dc in each of 4 sts on triangle, in ch 2 sp at top of triangle work 2 dc, ch 3, 2 dc, work dc in each of 4 foundation ch sts on triangle.

Side 2: Rep from * to ** (total 5 p shells, 4 V sts), in corner ch 3 sp work 4 sc, ch 3 and 4 sc. *Side 3:* Rep from ** to ** sp (6 p shells, 6 V sts), sl st top of turning ch 3, ch 3, turn.

Row 12:

Side 3: * 3 Dc in ch 3 sp of V st, ch 1, dc in sc of p shell, ch 1 ** rep from * across to corner shell, dc in each of 4 sc, 2 dc, ch 3 and 2 dc in ch 3 sp, dc in each of next 4 sc.

Side 2: Ch 1, dc in sc of p shell, ch 1, rep from * to ** across, dc next 6 dc, in ch 3 sp work 2 dc, ch 3, 2 dc, dc next 6 dc.

Side 1: Ch 1, dc in sc of p shell, ch 1, rep from * to ** across, dc next 4 dc, 2 dc, ch 3 and 2 dc in ch 3 sp, dc next 3 dc, sl st in turning ch 3. Fasten off. *Note:* Side 3 should total 48 sts between ch 3 corner sps; Side 2 should total 41 sts between corner ch 3 sps; Side 1 should total 65 sts between corner ch 3 sps. (Approximate measurements—Side 1, 10½″; Side 2, 12½″; Side 3, 15½″.)

Flower Triangle—Section C:

Make six. Work same as for section B substituting color G for color E in Rows 2 and 4, and color E for color G in Row 3.

UNIT 1:

(See Diagram 3), with H.

First Joining: To join △ B Side 3 to △ C Side 3 place △ C so that Side 3 is at top and flower to left. Holding △ B in same position place it on top of △ C. *Sides facing tog are right sides.* Join Side 3s as follows: ** Beg in corner ch 3 sps, sc in ch 3 sp on △ B, ch 1, sc in ch 3 sp on △ C; ch 1, sc next I st. On △ B, ch 1, sc next st on △ C; * ch 1, sk 2 sts on △ B, sc next st; ch 1, sk 2 sts on △ C, sc in next st; rep from * across ending in corner ch 3 sps. Fasten off.

Second Joining: Placing right sides together, join flower edge (2 Side 2s) of △ s just joined to top wing edge (side 1) of Section A. At seam on △ s count 2 ch 3 sps and 2 joining sc sts as 1 st each. Rep from ** on 1st joining.

Third Joining: To join △ C Side 1 to Section A Side 2, place 3 sections just joined, (right sides facing up) so that   s are at right and Side 2 of A is at top. Place △ C on top of Section A so that Side 1 is at top and Side 2 (flower) is at *right*. Rep from ** on 1st joining, substituting top of ch 12 for end corner ch 3 sp.

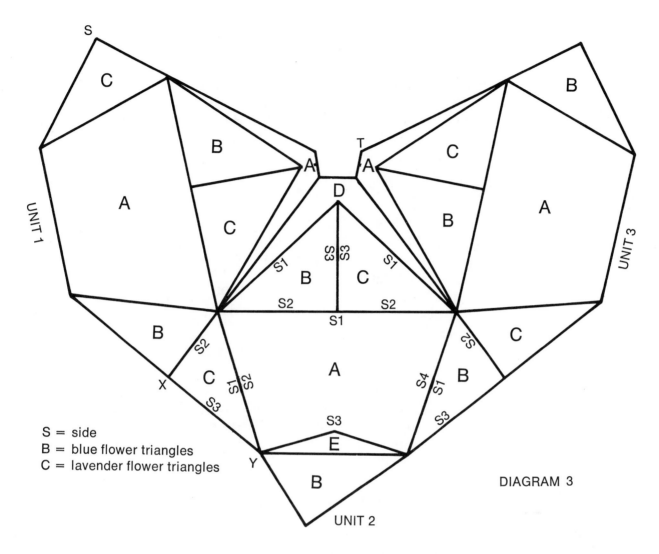

S = side
B = blue flower triangles
C = lavender flower triangles

DIAGRAM 3

Fourth Joining: To join △ B Side 1 to Section A Side 2, place 4 sections just joined (right sides facing up) so that joined △ s are at left and Side 4 of Section A is at top. Place △ B on top of Section A so that Side 1 is on top and Side 2 (flower) is at *left.* Rep from ** on 1st joining substituting top of ch 12 for beg ch 3 sp. (Check to be sure all joinings are worked on the wrong side.)

Unit Edging: Area D: (See Diagram 3.) With H, place unit so that butterfly is at bottom, right side facing you. Beg on bottom △ B at X on Diagram 3. Sc in ch 3 sp, sc each st across edge of △ B to ch 3 sp, work 3 trc in ch 3 sp, sk seam dtrc in corner ch 3 sp on Section A, sk seam, 3 trc in ch 3 sp on next triangle, skipping ch 1 sps (dec), work sc across to within last 10 sts before ch 3 sp, dc next st, trc next 6 sts, 3 trc, ch 3 and 3 trc in next st, sk 2 sts, work 3 dc in ch 3 sp, sk seam, work 3 dc in ch

3 sp of next triangle, sk 2 sts, 3 trc, ch 3 and 3 trc in next st, trc next 6 sts, dc next st; skipping ch 1 sps, sc across to ch 3 sp at end of triangle, 3 trc in ch 3 sp, sk seam, dtrc in corner ch 3 sp on Section A, sk seam, 3 trc in ch 3 sp of next triangle, sc in each st across, end sc in ch 3 sp. Fasten off.

UNIT 2 AND UNIT 3:

Worked same as for Unit 1.

Area E: (See Diagram 3 for position.)

Row 1: With H, wk on Unit 2, *right side facing you.* Place unit so that Side 3 of Section A is on top (bottom wing edge). Beg in ch 12 sp (Y on diagram), work 12 sc in ch 12 sp, dc next 10 sts, dtrc next 6 sts, tr trc next 6 sts, (quint dc holding back last lp on hk in next st) three times, yo, pull through all 4 lps on hk (cluster made), sk 2 sts, quint dc next st, sk 2 sts, cluster, tr trc next 6 sts, dtrc next 6 sts, dc next 10 sts, 12 sc over ch 12 sp. Fasten off. *Do not turn.*

Row 2: Sk first 3 sts on Row 1, sc next 3 sts, hdc next 6 sts, dc next 16 sts, trc next 5 sts, dtrc next 7 sts, trc next 5 sts, dc next 16 sts, hdc next 6 sts, sc next 3 sts. Fasten off. Join △ B Side 1 to this edge. With right side of Section A facing △ B and flower to the left, join with overcast st working *back* lps only.

Joining Units: With H (see Diagram 3 for placements). With right sides facing, join Unit 1 to Unit 2. Beg in ch 3 sp at bottom edge (X on diagram). Rep 1st joining from **. Join Unit 3 to Unit 2 in the same manner.

Fringe: With H, beg at S on Diagram 3. Sc in ch 3 sp on bottom edge, * ch 5, sk 3 sts, sc next st, rep from * across bottom. Fasten off. To make one tassel, cut seven 30″ lengths. Hold lengths tog and fold in half. Draw folded end through ch 5 lp from back to front, draw ends through fold and pull tight. Work 1 tassel in each lp around.

Neck Edging and Ties: With H, use double strand. Ch 6, * work 4 dc in 3rd ch st from hk, 4 dc in each of next 2 sts, sl st in next ch st, * ch 87; working on neck edge, right side facing you, beg at T on diagram, sc in ch 3 sp, sl st to ch 3 sp at seam; work sc over ch 3 sp, sc in each of next 2 joining sc, sc next ch 3 sp; cont sl st around, working second seam in same manner as first, end sc in end ch 3 sp, ch 80, rep from * to *. Fasten off.

Patchwork Hanging

Size:

35" × 44".

Materials:

Knitting worsted-weight yarn. Use double strands throughout.

Pale Dusty Pink	1 skein (4-oz. each)
Celery Green	1 skein
Beige	1 skein
Pale Rust	1 skein
Light Forest Green	1 skein
Hunter Green	1 skein
Dark Tan	1 skein
Dark Forest Green	2 skeins (4-oz. each)
Pale Lavender	2 skeins (4-oz. each)
Cranberry	2 skeins (4-oz. each)
Jade Green	2 skeins (4-oz. each)
Light Orange	2 oz.
Buttercup Yellow	2 oz.
Emerald Green	2 oz.
Sky Blue	2 oz.
Dark Lavender	2 oz.
Dark Dusty Pink	2 oz.

Two dowels, each ½" diameter and 35" long.

Hook:

Size H aluminum or size to obtain gauge.

Gauge:

4 dc = 1".

Central Area:

STRIPE HEXAGON A:

Make twelve.

Round 1: Use Light Forest Green. Ch 6, join with sl st to form ring. Ch 3, work 11 dc in ring, sl st top ch st of beg. ch 3. Fasten off. Turn.

Round 2: Use Pale Dusty Rose. Work 2 hdc in each st around, sl st beg hdc, ch 2, turn.

Round 3: Work sc in each of next 2 sts, * in next st work sc, ch 2, and sc, ** sc in each of next 3 sts, rep from * four times, rep from * to **, sl st top of beg ch 2. Fasten off. *Do not turn.*

Round 4: Use Celery. (*Mark side facing you as the right side.*) Beg in any ch 2 sp. * Work sc, ch 2 and sc in ch 2 sp, sc in each of next 5 sc, rep from * five times, sl st beg sc. Fasten off.

Round 5: Use Hunter Green. Beg in any ch 2 sp. *Work sc, ch 2 and sc in ch 2 sp, *working back lps only* sc in each of next 7 sts, rep from * five times, sl st beg sc. Fasten off.

Round 6: Use Celery. Beg in any ch 2 sp. * Work sc, ch 2 and sc in ch 2 sp, *working back lps only*, sc in each of next 9 sts, rep from * five times, sl st beg sc. Fasten off.

FLOWER HEXAGON B:

Make eight.

Round 1: Use Beige. Ch 6, join with sl st to form ring. Ch 2, work 11 sc in ring, sl st top ch 2. Fasten off.

Round 2: Use Cranberry. Beg in any st. * Work 2 sc, 1 sc next st, rep from * around (total 18 sts), sl st beg st. Fasten off.

Round 3: Use Beige. Beg in any st. * Work sc in each of next 3 sts, ch 6, (foundation ch) sc in 4th ch st from hk, trc next st, sc next st, (petal formed,) rep from * five times, sl st in 2 beg sc.

Round 4: * Sk next sc, working around petal, sc in next ch st (of foundation ch), 3 dc next st, sc next st, in ch 3 sp at tip of work, sc, ch 2 and sc, sc next st, 3 dc next st, sc next st, sk next st, sl st next st, rep from * five times. Fasten off.

Round 5: Use Cranberry. Beg at tip of petal in first of 2 ch sts. *Work back lps only.* * Sc in first ch st, ch 2, sc in next ch st, sc in each of next 4 sts, sk 2 sts: Work long dc (ldc) between petals as follows: yo, insert hk in base of previous row st, pull through long lp, continue to work as for dc; sk 2 sts, work sc in each of next 4 sts, rep from * five times, sl st beg sc. Fasten off.

Round 6: Use Rust. Beg in any ch 2 tip. * Work sc, ch 2 and sc in ch 2 sp, sc next st, hdc in each of next 2 sts, dc next st, (sk 1 st, dc next st) twice, hdc in each of next 2 sts, sc next st, rep from * five times. Sl st in beg sc. Fasten off.

SOLID HEXAGON C:

Make seven, one each in Cranberry Red, Bright Orange, Buttercup Yellow, Emerald Green, Sky Blue, Dark Lavender, and Dark Dusty Pink.

Round 1: Ch 6, join with sl st to form ring, ch 3, work 11 dc in ring, sl st top ch 3, ch 3, turn.

Round 2: Work dc in sm sp as turning ch, work 2 dc in each st around, sl st top ch 3, ch 3, turn (total 24 sts counting turning ch).

Round 3: *Work back lps only*, dc sm sp as turning ch, * dc next st, 2 dc next st, rep from * around, ending dc last st, sl st top of ch 3, ch 2, turn.

Round 4: *Work side facing you now as right side. Work back lps only.* In sm sp as turning ch work hdc, ch 2, 2 hdc, * hdc in each of next 5 sts, ** 2 hdc, ch 2, 2 hdc in next st, rep from * four times, rep from * to **, sl st top of ch 2, ch 2, do not turn.

Round 5: Work hdc next st, * in ch 2 sp work sc, ch 2 and sc, ** hdc in each of next 9 sts, rep from * four times, rep from * to **, hdc in each of next 7 sts, sl st top ch 2. Fasten off.

HALF HEXAGON D:

Row 1: Use Dark Forest Green. Ch 5, join with sl st in beg ch st to form ring; ch 3, 6 dc in ring, ch 3, turn.

Row 2: Dc sm sp as turning ch, 2 dc in each st across (total 14 sts counting turning ch), ch 3, turn.

Row 3: Dc sm sp as turning ch, * dc next st, 2 dc next st, rep from * across ending 1 dc in top of ch 3 (total 21 sts), ch 2, turn.

Row 4: *Work back lps only.* Hdc in each of next 6 sts, 2 hdc, ch 2 and 2 hdc in next st, hdc in each of next 5 sts, 2 hdc, ch 2 and 2 hdc in next st, hdc in each of next 7 sts, ch 2, turn.

Row 5: 2 Sc in sm sp as turning ch, sc in each of next 8 sts, in ch 2 sp work sc, ch 2 and sc, sc in each of next 9 sts, in ch 2 sp work sc, ch 2 and sc, sc in each of next 8 sts, 2 sc in top of ch 2.

Row 6: (Edging unfinished edge). Ch 2, sc over ch 2 sp, 2 sc over each of next 3 end-of-row sts, sk center of beg ring, 2 sc in each of next 3 end-of-row sts, sc over hdc st, ch 2, sl st top of ch 2. Fasten off.

Joining: See diagram on page 167 for position of hexagons. With wrong sides facing sl st all hexagons together working back lps only.

Note: Each side of hexagon has 13 sts (ch 1, 11 sts, ch 1).

Ground:

AREA E:

Round 1: Use Dark Forest Green. Begin at X on diagram. *Work back lps only.*

Side 1: Beg in sc *before* ch 2 sp at tip of C hexagon, sc, ** [ch 2, sk 2 ch sts, sc next st, hdc in next 3 sts, dc next 3 sts, holding back last lps on hk work trc in next 3 sts, yo, pull through all 4 lps on hk (3 trc cluster made). Holding back last lps on hk work dtrc in next 2 sts, sk seam, beg in ch st, wk dtrc in next 2 sts still holding back last lps on hk, yo, pull through all 5 lps on hk, (4 dtrc cluster made), work 3 trc cluster over next 3 sts, dc in next 3 sts, hdc in next 3 sts, sc next st] ch 2, sk ch 2 sp, sc next 11 sts, sc in ch 1 st, sk seam, sc in ch st on next hexagon, sc next 14 sc, sc in ch 1 st, sk seam, sc in ch st on next hexagon, sc next 11 sc, rep [ ].

Side 2: * Ch 2, sk 2 sts, sc next 11 sts *, rep [ ] four times, rep from * to *.

Side 3: Rep Side 1 from **.

Side 4: * Ch 2, sk 2 sts, sc next 11 sts, rep [ ] four times, ch 2, sk 2 sts, sc next 10 sts, sl st beg sc, ch 2, turn.

Round 2: * Hdc next 10 sts, in ch 2 sp work hdc, ch 2 and hdc (shell) *place markers in ch 2 sp of every shell made.* (hdc next 17 sts, ch 2, sk 2 ch sts) three times, hdc next 17 sts, work shell in next ch 2 sp, hdc next 11 sts, ch 2, sk 2 ch sts, hdc next 17 sts, shell in next ch 2 sp, hdc next 40 sts, shell in next ch 2 sp, hdc next 17 sts, ch 2, sk ch 2 sp, ** hdc next st, rep from * to **, sl st in top of beg ch 2, ch 2, do not turn.

Round 3: Rep Rnd 2. *Work back lps only.* Hdc each st except ch 2 over each ch 2 sp and work shell in each shell removing markers as you go.

Note: place marker in ch 2 sp of last shell made.

Border:

Round 1: Use Pale Lavender. Turn piece so that right side is facing you. Start at marker (see Y in diagram). *Work back lps only.*

Top: In hdc after ch 2 sp, ** [sc, sk 3 sts, 4 trc in next st, ch 5, sc in 5th ch st from hk (picot-p), 4 trc in next st, sk next 3 sts, sc next 2 sts] four times.

Corner: * In ch 2 sp of shell work 3 trc, p and 3 trc, sk next hdc, * including ch sts, rep [ ] three times, rep from * to *,

Side: Sk next st, including ch sts rep [ ] seven times, rep corner; you are now at bottom of piece, rep from **, sl st beg st. Fasten off.

Round 2: Use Jade Green. *Right side facing you.* Beg in last shell made. *Work back lps only.* Beg in trc after p, sc, sk 2 trc, 3 trc next st; **

Top: [Sk 2 trc, sc next 2 trc, ch 2, sk p, sc next 2 trc, sk 2 trc, 2 trc next sc, trc next sc, 2 trc next sc] four times, omit last 2 trc on 4th rep.

Corner: * Sk 2 trc, sc next trc, ch 2, sk p, sc next trc, place marker in ch 2 sp just made, sk 2 trc, 3 trc next st, * rep [ ] three times, omit last 2 trc on 3rd rep:

Side: Rep [ ] seven times, omit last 2 trc on 8th rep **.

Corner: Rep from * to *, rep remainder of rnd from ** to **, sk 2 trc, sc next trc, ch 2, sl st beg st, ch 2, turn.

Round 3: In ea ch 2 sp with marker work dc, ch 2, dc, replacing marker in ch 2 sp just made. Work dc in each trc and sc sts and ch 2 over each ch 2 sp, sl st top of turning ch 2. Fasten off.

Round 4: Use Cranberry. Turn piece so that right side is facing you. *Work back lps only.* Beg in second st to *left* of break-off st. ** *Top:* [sc next st, sk 3 sts, 4 trc in next ch st, ch 5, sc in 5th ch st from hk (picot-p) 4 trc in next ch st, sk 3 sts, sc next 2 sts] four times; Corner: sk 2 sts * in ch 2 sp work 3 trc, p, 3 trc, sk 3 sts, * rep [ ] three times, sk 2 sts, rep from * to *. Side: Rep [ ] seven times; rep corner; rep from **, sl st top of beg sc. Fasten off.

Round 5: Use Dark Tan. Right side facing you, beg in last shell made. *Work back lps only.* Beg at break-off st. **

Top: [Sk 2 trc, sc next 2 trc, ch 2, sk p, sc next 2 trc, sk 2 trc, 2 trc next sc, trc next sc, 2 trc next sc] four times omit last 2 trc on 4th rep.

Corner: * Sk 1 trc, sc next 2 trc, ch 2, sk p, sc next trc, *place marker in ch 2 sp just made, sk 2 trc, 3 trc next st, * rep [ ] three times, omit last 2 trc on 3rd rep.

Side; rep [ ] seven times, omit last 2 trc on 7th rep; rep corner; remainder of rnd rep from **, sl st beg sc, ch 2, turn.

Corners: Triangle: Beg in any corner (see F on diagram).

Row 1: Use Pale Lavender. Right side facing you, start at marker to your right. Sk 7 sts, in ch 2 sp work sc, *working back lps only* sc next 20 sts, sc in next ch 2 sp, ch 2, turn.

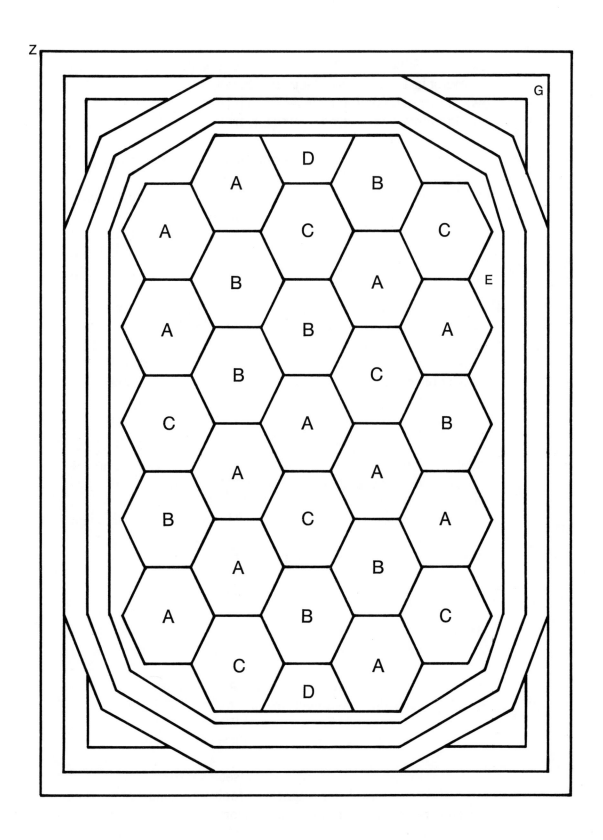

Row 2: Work both lps. Work next 2 sc as one (dec), sc across end working last 2 sc as one (dec), ch 2, turn.
Rows 3 through 10: Rep Row 2.
Row 11: Work next 2 sc as one, sc end st. Fasten off.

Triangle Outline (see G on diagram): Use Jade Green. Right side facing you, beg in ch 2 sp with marker on the right.
Row 1: Sc in ch 2 sp with marker, *working back lps only* sc next 5 sts, in next ch 2 sp work 4 dc, sk first row of triangle, work sc over next 10 end-of-row sts, in tip of triangle, work sc, ch 2 and sc, work sc over next 10 end-of-row sts, sk next row, 4 dc in ch 2 sp, sk 2 sts, *working back lps only* sc next 5 sts, sc in ch 2 sp with marker, ch 2, turn.
Row 2: Work next 2 sc as one (dec), sc next st, sk 2 sts, * wk 2 dc next st, dc next 2 sts *, rep from * to * to tip of triangle; in ch 2 sp work dc, ch 2 and dc, rep from * to * through 4 dc, sk 2 sc, sc next 2 sc, work last 2 sc as one (dec). Each side should have 24 sts not counting ch 2. Fasten off. Rep for rem 3 corners.

FINAL BORDER:

Round 1: Use Cranberry. *Work back lps only*. Beg at Z on diagram. * In ch 2 sp work 4 trc, p, and 4 trc, sk 3 sts, sc next 4 sts; [sk 3 sts, 4 trc next st, p, 4 trc next st, sk 3 sts, sc next 3 sts] twice; (Note: on last rep, last 3 sts skipped are last st on triangle, ch sp and next sc after p), rep [ ] nine times; sc next st; sk 3 sts, in ch 2 sp work 4 trc, p, and 4 trc, sk 3 sts, sc next 4 sts; rep [ ] eight times, sc next st; rep from * sl st beg trc. Fasten off.

FINISHING:

Attaching Dowel: Work on wrong side at top edge. Fold top 2½" over toward front (2½" measuring from p st). Along folded edge work series of lps as follows: sc in fold at ½" from side edge, ch 6, sc 1¼" away from last sc. Work in pattern to within ½" of next side. Weave dowel through lps back to front.

Arlene Mintzer

*In the world of crochet, Arlene Mintzer wears many hats:
designer for major magazines, free-lance instruction writer for
both magazines and yarn companies, maker of garments and
other crocheted objects for galleries and boutiques, and teacher.
The magazines Arlene designs for include Woman's Day, Good
Housekeeping Needlecraft, Ladies' Home Journal Needle & Craft,
and American Home Crafts. Much of her time, when she isn't
designing, is spent teaching. At New York's Village Weaving Center in Greenwich Village, Arlene conducts a beginning crochet
class, an advanced crochet class, a creative crochet workshop, a
beginning knitting class, and an advanced knitting class.*

"When I begin working on a new design, I start by sitting down with a whole group of yarns in different colors—colors that really please me. While I do have some idea of what I want to do before I start, I find that sitting down with my materials before helps me to turn that idea into a finished design.

"I think that crocheters who read the magazines I design for are looking for something interesting to make, especially experienced crocheters who are looking for more than just another plain garment. What they want is something that's going to be a challenge. I do a lot of teaching and when my students see for the first time what exciting things can be made with a crochet hook, it brings out all their creative energy.

"I, too, was once a beginner who needed to be shown the way, and luckily I came into contact with some people who gave me advice that I still cherish to this day. Ruth Jacksier of **Woman's Day,** for one, was very patient in explaining a lot of things about crochet. 'You can do anything with anything,' she told me, which I took to mean that the most important rule for creativity is flexibility."

Arlene Mintzer

Capelet and Skirt

Capelet

Size:

One size will fit Small, Medium, and Large.

Materials:

You will need worsted-weight tweed-type yarn in the following colors and amounts:

Pale Lavender (A)	3 ozs.
Medium Pink (B)	2 ozs.
Grape (C)	2 ozs.
Medium Rose (D)	2 ozs.
Raspberry (E)	2 ozs.
Medium Purple (F)	2 ozs.

Brushed wool mohair, Beige (G), 3 ozs.
Medium-weight cotton yarn, Light Pink (H)
    and Magenta (I), 3 ozs. each.
Very fine-weight yarn, Medium Pink (J), 2 oz.

Hooks:

Sizes G and E aluminum or sizes to obtain gauge.

Gauge:

G hook, 7 dc = 2″; 2 dc and 1 sc row = 2″.

Starting at neck edge with A and G hook, ch 55 to measure approx 15″.

Row 1 (right side): Dc in 4th ch from hook and in each ch across (53 dc). Change to G. Fasten off A. Ch 1, turn.

Note: Ch 3 counts as 1 dc. Ch 1 *does not* count as 1 sc.

Row 2: With G, sc in front lp of each st across. Change to F. Fasten off G. Ch 3, turn.

Row 3 (increase row): With F, dc in back lp of first st (1 st inc), * dc in next st, 2 dc in next st. Rep from * across (79 dc). Drop lp from hook. Place safety pin in lp to prevent st from slipping.

Dark Picot Edge Row (DPER): With 1 strand each of I and J held tog and right side facing you, sc in first unworked lp of last G row, * sc in next lp, ch 2, sc in same lp (picot made), sc in next lp. Rep from * across. Fasten off.
Remove safety pin from dropped F lp and place st on hook. Ch 3, turn.

Row 4: Skip first st (Remember ch 3 counts as 1 st), dc in each remaining st across (79 dc). Change to G. Fasten off F. Ch 1, turn.

Row 5: Working in back lp, sc in each st across. Change to A. Ch 3, turn.

Row 6 (increase row): Skip first st, working in front lp, dc in next st, 2 dc in next st, * dc in each of next 2 dc, 2 dc in next st. Rep from * ending dc in last st (105 dc). Drop lp from hook as before.

Light Picot Edge Row (LPER): Work as for DPER using 1 strand each of H and J held tog. Fasten off. Pick up dropped lp. Ch 3, turn.

Row 7: Skip first st, work a dc in back lp of each st across. Change to G. Ch 1, turn.

Row 8: Sc in front lp of each st across. Change to B.

Row 9 (increase row): Skip first st, working in back lp, dc in each of next 2 sts, 2 dc in next st, * dc in each of next 3 sts, 2 dc in next st. Rep from * ending dc in last st (131 dc). Drop lp from hook as before.
Work a DPER across last G Row.
Pick up dropped lp. Ch 3, turn.

Row 10: Dc across. Change to G. Ch 1, turn.

Row 11: Rep Row 5. Change to C.

Row 12 (increase row): Skip first st, working in front lp, dc in each of next 4 sts, 2 dc in next st, * dc in each of next 5 sts, 2 dc in next st. Rep from * ending dc in each of last 5 dc (152 dc). Drop lp from hook as before.
Work a LPER across last G Row.
Pick up dropped lp. Ch 3, turn.

Row 13: Rep Row 7. Change to G.

Row 14: Rep Row 2. Change to D.

Row 15 (increase row): Skip first st, working in back lp, dc in each of next 6 sts, 2 dc in next st, * dc in each of next 7 sts, 2 dc in next st. Rep from * across to within last 8 sts, dc in each remaining st (170 dc). Drop lp from hook as before.

Work a DPER across last G Row.

Pick up dropped lp. Ch 3, turn.

Row 16: Rep Row 10. Change to G. Ch 1, turn.

Row 17: Rep Row 5. Change to A.

Row 18 (increase row): Skip first st, working in front lp, dc in each of next 8 sts, 2 dc in next st, * dc in each of next 9 sts, 2 dc in next st. Rep from * across to within last 10 sts, dc in each remaining st (186 dc). Drop lp from hook as before.

Work a LPER across last G Row.

Pick up dropped lp. Ch 3, turn.

Row 19: Rep Row 7. Change to G. Ch 1, turn.

Row 20: Rep Row 2. Change to E.

Row 21 (increase row): Skip first st, working in back lp dc in each of next 14 sts, 2 dc in next st, * dc in each of next 15 sts, 2 dc in next st. Rep from * across to within last 10 sts, dc in each remaining st (197 dc). Drop lp from hook as before.

Work a DPER across last G Row.

Pick up dropped lp.

Row 22: Rep Row 10. Change to G. Ch 1, turn.

Row 23: Rep Row 2. Change to A. Ch 3, turn.

Row 24: Rep Row 10. Drop lp from hook as before.

Work a LPER across last G Row.

Pick up dropped lp. Ch 3, turn.

Row 25: Skip first st, dc in front lp of each st across. Change to G. Ch 1, turn.

Row 26: Rep Row 5. Change to F. Ch 3, turn.

Row 27: Rep Row 25. Change to D. Ch 3, turn.

Row 28: Rep Row 10. Fasten off.

Work a DPER across last G Row.

Work a LPER across last F Row.

Neck Edging: Work a LPER along opposite side of starting chain at neck edge.

Body Edging: Work a DPER along front and lower edges of capelet, making sure to have the same number of sts on each front and spacing them as evenly as possible.

TIES:

Work with 2 strands of cotton held tog, starting at one end of tie, use H and Size E hook. Ch 13. Working *tightly*, work 4 sc in

2nd ch from hook, * work 4 sc in next ch. Rep from * across next 11 sc (spiral completed). With lp still on hook work a chain about 6" long, ch 13, work 4 sc in 2nd ch from hook. Rep from * across next 11 sc. Fasten off. Make 4 more H ties and 5 I ties. Pull one spiral end of each tie through front edges of capelet in desired color sequence, following photo for placement.

Skirt

Size:

Directions are for small size. Changes for Medium and Large are in parentheses.

Materials:

Same as for capelet in the following amounts:

Pale Lavender (A)	5 ozs.
Medium Pink (B)	2 ozs.
Grape (C)	2 ozs.
Medium Rose (D)	6 ozs.
Raspberry (E)	2 ozs.
Medium Purple (F)	2 ozs.
Light Pink (H)	2 ozs.
Magenta (I)	2 ozs.
Medium Pink (J)	4 ozs.

Hook:

Sizes G and F aluminum or sizes to obtain gauge.

Gauge:

G hook, 7 dc = 2", 2 rows = 2".

Measurement:

Garment will fit a 24" to 26" (28" to 30") waist with an adjustable drawstring waistband. Garment will fit a 33" to 35" (37" to 39") hip.

Note: Skirt is worked from top down in one piece.
Starting at waist edge with size G hook and D ch 93 (107) sts to measure about 26" (30").

Round 1: Dc in 4th ch from hook and in each ch across, 91 (105) dc. Join with sl st to top of ch 3, being careful not to twist.
Note: Ch 3 always counts as 1 dc.

Note: It is advisable that as you work, you try skirt on to ensure an accurate fit.

DRAWSTRING:

With double strand of H and size F hook, ch 13. Working tightly, work 4 sc in 2nd ch from hook, * work 4 sc in next ch. Rep from * across next 11 sc (spiral completed). With lp still on hook, work a chain to measure approx 44" (46") long, ch 13, work 4 sc in 2nd ch from hook. Rep from * across next 11 ch. Fasten off. Weave drawstring in and out of Round 1.
Note: Work in back lp of each st until otherwise specified.

Round 2: Ch 3, dc in each of next 21 (25) sts, * 2 dc in next st (1 st inc). Place a marker in either of these 2 sts, * dc in each of next 46 (52) sts. Rep from * to *, dc in each of the remaining 21 (25) sts. Join with a sl st to ch 3, 93 (107) sts.

Round 3: Ch 3, dc in each st to marked st, * 2 dc in marked st, dc in each dc to next marked st, 2 dc in next marked st, dc in each remaining st. Join 95 (109) dc. Continue to inc 2 sts each rnd at side edges three times more. 101 (115) sts.

Note: Remember to move markers each round. Always join each round with a slip stitch.

Round 7: Ch 3, * dc in each dc to within dc before marked dc, 2 dc in this st, 2 dc in marked st (4 dc group made with 2 increased sts.) Rep from * once more, ending dc in each remaining st. 105 (119) sts.

Round 8: Ch 3, inc 1 st at each side edge as before, working increases in 3rd dc of 4 dc group. 107 (121) sts.

Rounds 9 and 10: Inc 1 st at each side edge as before, 111 (125) sts.

Round 11: Rep Rnd 7, 115 (129) sts.

Round 12: Rep Rnd 8, 117 (131) sts.

Round 13: Rep Rnd 7, 121 (135) sts.
Work even in dc pattern for 3 rnds. Change to G.

BODY PATTERN:

Round 1: Ch 1, sc in same place as sl st, working in back lp, sc in each st around. Change to A. Sl st to first sc, Fasten off G.
Note: Ch 1 does not count as 1 sc.

Round 2: Ch 3, dc in back lp of each st around. Join.

Round 3: Ch 3, dc in each st around. Change to G. Drop lp from hook. Place safety in lp to prevent st from slipping.

With F hook, work a DPER across last G rnd. Join Fasten off. Remove safety pin from dropped lp and place st on hook.

Round 4: Rep Rnd 1. Change to F.

Rounds 5 and 6: Rep Rnds 2 and 3.

With F hook, work a LPER across last G round. Join. Always work each DPER and LPER with F hook. Continue to repeat these 3 rounds, always working first round with G and every 2nd and 3rd round in the following color sequence: A, B, C, D, A, E, A, F, B, C, D, A, and E.

Note: Skirt measures 36" from waist to lower edge when completed. Skirt may be made shorter or longer as desired, merely by subtracting or adding rounds. Continue to alternate a DPER and LPER on G rounds as before, leaving last 4 G rounds unworked.

Edging Rounds: Work a DPER in front lp of each st on last rnd. Change to G. Next Round: With G, sc in back lp of each st of last rnd. Fasten off. Following Round: Work a LPER in front lp of each G sc of last rnd.

Popcorn Vest

Size:

This garment will fit a 32″ to 36″ bust measurement.

Materials:

Tweed-type worsted-weight yarn

Blue-Gray (A)	12 ozs.

3-strand Persian-type needlepoint and crewel yarn in the following colors:

Dark Rust (B)	2 ozs.
Beige (C)	2 ozs.
Apricot (D)	2 ozs.
Aqua (E)	2 ozs.
Light Rust (F)	2 ozs.
Light Aqua (G)	2 ozs.

6 Buttons, 1″ in diameter.

Hook:

Size H aluminum or size to obtain gauge.

Gauge:

7 sc = 2″, 6 shell pattern rows = 2½″.

LOWER BORDER:

Starting at lower edge with B, ch 122 to measure 35″.

Note: Vest is worked in one piece to underarms.

Row 1 (right side): Sc in 2nd ch from hookacross (121) sts). Ch 1, turn.

Row 2 (popcorn row): Sc in each of first 2 sc, work popcorn in next sc as follows: (yo hook, draw up a lp in same st, yo, draw thru 2 lps on hook) five times, yo, draw through all 6 lps on hook, ch 1 (popcorn made), * sc in each of next 3 sc, work popcorn in next st. Rep from * across, ending sc in each of last 2 sc. Ch 1, turn.

Row 3: Sc in each sc and popcorn across. Fasten off B. *Do not turn.*

Row 4: Make lp on hook with C. With same side still facing you, draw up a lp in first sc, yo, draw through both lps (sc completed). Sc in each remaining sc across row. Ch 1, turn.

Row 5: Work in popcorn pattern across. Ch 1, turn.

Row 6: Work even in sc. Fasten off C. Turn.

Row 7: Make lp on hook with D, sc in each sc across. Ch 1, turn.

Row 8: Work across in popcorn pattern. Ch 1, turn.

Row 9: Work a sc in each sc and popcorn across. *Do not turn.*

Rows 10 through 15: Rep Rows 4 through 9, working 3 rows each in E and F.

Rows 16 and 17: Rep Rows 4 and 5 with G. Fasten off.

Note: Remainder of body is worked with A only.

BODY PATTERN, FOUNDATION ROW:

With right side facing you, sl st to first G sc, ch 3, work 2 dc in this sc, skip next sc and the popcorn st, sc in next sc, * skip next 2 sts, work 5 dc in next st (shell made). Sk next 2 sts, 2 scs in next st. Rep from * to last 6 sts, skip 2 sts, sc in next st, skip 2 sts, 3 dc in last st. Ch 3, turn.

Row 1: Skip first 3 dc, * sc in next sc, ch 2, sc in 3rd dc of shell, ch 2. Rep from * ending last repeat, sc in top of ch 3. Turn.

Row 2: Sc in first sc, * work a shell in next sc, sc in next sc. Rep from * ending sc in bottom of ch 3. Ch 3, turn.

Row 3: Sc in 3rd dc of first shell, * ch 2 in next sc, ch 2, sc in 3rd dc of next shell. Rep from * ending sc in last sc, ch 3, turn.

Row 4: Work 2 dc in first sc, * sc in next sc, work shell in next sc. Rep from * ending last repeat with 3 dc in bottom of ch 3. Ch 3, turn. (At end of this row you should have 19 full shells and 2 half-shells on each end.)

Repeat these 4 rows for pattern until piece measures about 13″ or desired length from beg, ending with a 4th pattern row.

To Divide for Fronts and Back:

RIGHT FRONT:

Row 1: Work in pattern as established across first 3 full shells, sc in 3rd dc of 4th shell (mark this sc). Ch 3, turn.

Rows 2 through 4: Work in pattern across.

Repeat these 4 rows until piece measures 5″ from beg, ending with a 4th row. Do not ch at end of last row. Turn.

180

To Shape Neck:

Row 1: Sl st across 6 sts, sc in 3rd dc of next shell. Continue across in pattern, turn.

Row 2: Work in pattern across, ending sc in last sc. Ch 3, turn.

Row 3: Sl st in 3rd dc of first shell, continue across in pattern, ch 3, turn.

Row 4: Work in pattern across, ending shell in last sc (sl st is not worked into). Ch 3, turn.

Row 5: Sl st in 3rd dc of first shell and next sc, ch 2, continue across in pattern. Turn.

Continue to work even in pattern if necessary until armhole measures 7″ from beg. Fasten off.

BACK:

Go back to original dividing row. With wrong side of piece facing you, skip marked sc and next shell, then sc in 3rd dc of next shell. Work in pattern across next 7 shells, ending with a sc in 3rd dc of next shell (mark this st). Work in pattern until back measures same as front to shoulder. Fasten off.

LEFT FRONT:

Go back to original dividing row. Skip marked st and next shell, then sc in next shell. Work in pattern across remaining sts to correspond to right front reversing all shaping. Sew shoulder seams.

SLEEVES:

With G, ch 50 to measure about 14″.

Note: Sleeves are worked from the top down. It is important that they fit properly in the armhole. I advise you to work about 4 rows in pattern; fold sleeve in half, placing chain edge against arm edge to make sure pieces are flush.

Row 1: Sc in 2nd ch from hook and in each ch across. Ch 1, turn.

Row 2: Sc in each of first 2 sc, work popcorn in next st, * sc in each of next 3 sc, work popcorn in next sc. Rep from * across, ending sc in each of last 2 sc. Fasten off. Turn.

Row 3: With F, make lp on hook, sc in each sc and popcorn. Ch 1, turn.

Row 4: Rep Row 2. Fasten off. Turn.

Repeat these last 2 rows three times more, working 2 rows each D, C, and B.

Left Front Border:

Row 1: With A and right side facing you, work a row of sc along front edge. Ch 1, turn.

Row 2: Sc in each sc across. Ch 1, turn.

Row 3: Mark edge for 4 buttonholes, the first about 3″ from lower edge, the last about ½″ from neck edge, the others evenly spaced between. Sc in each sc across to first marker, ch 3, skip 3 sc, sc in each sc across to next marker. Rep from * across, ending sc in each remaining sc. Ch 1, turn.

Row 4: Sc in each sc and ch for buttonholes. Fasten off.

Right Border: Work to correspond to left border omitting buttonholes. Fasten off.

Body Edging: With A and right side facing you, sc in each sc of front border edges and around neck edge. Fasten off.

Sleeve Edging: With A and right side of sleeve facing you, sc in each st along opposite side of starting chain. Fasten off.

Finishing: Sew in sleeves. Sew sleeve seams. Sew on buttons.

Man's or Woman's
Long Jacket and Scarf

Long Jacket

Size:

Directions will fit men's chest sizes 36" to 42". Women's bust sizes 32" to 38" will be found in parentheses. Finished jacket measures 44" (40") with a 1" border added to each front.

Materials:

You will need approx 61 ozs. of yarn to complete the jacket and scarf.

A total of 11 ozs. tweed-type worsted-weight yarn in 3 colors: Dark Brown, Blue, and Light Rust.

A total of 10 ozs. in brushed mohair yarn in 5 colors: Pale Peach, Light Cocoa, Light Rust, Moss Green, and Magenta.

A total of 10 ozs. in variegated medium-weight yarn in 2 colors: shades of Turquoise and Green/Blue/Gold combination.

A total of *4 ozs. heavy-weight looped mohair yarn in 2 colors: Medium Aqua and Dark Aqua.

A total of 3 ozs. very thick novelty yarn in 1 color: shades of Rust/Brown and Orange/Green variegated combination.

A total of * 3 ozs. lightweight looped mohair in 1 color: Pale Aqua/Magenta.

A total of 9 ozs. knitting worsted-type yarn in 4 colors: Turquoise, Lavender, Moss Green, and Red.

A total of * 3 ozs. worsted-weight alpaca yarn in Moss Green.

A total of * 3 ozs. variegated knitting worsted-weight yarn in shades of Orange.

A total of 3 ozs. bulky-weight in Gold.

A total of 2 oz. nubbed bulky in Tan.

Note: The * yarns above were dyed with chemical dyes that work well on natural fibers such as mohair, alpaca, and of course my favorite, wool. If you are looking for just the right shade and can't seem to find it, you might want to investigate the process. It's a lot of fun and doesn't require much space or fancy materials.

This jacket is a great project for all those leftover yarns you never knew what to do with. The above are just a suggestion for you.

Hook:

Size K aluminum or size to obtain gauge.

Gauge:

2 sc = 1″.

Note: It is important that your gauge be accurate to ensure a proper-fitting garment. Since you will be working with many different weights of yarn it is best to work about 6 or 8 sts in that specific combination; measure these sts and see if you're getting the proper gauge. If you're getting fewer than 2 sts to 1″ then you must add strand(s) of yarn. If you are getting more than 2 sts to 1″, then you must subtract strand(s) of yarn. Jacket is worked in one piece to underarms.

LOWER BORDER:

The lower border edge of this jacket was worked with a very thick handspun yarn. Because the yarn was so thick and could not actually be crocheted, the best way to have used it effectively was to crochet over it using the following techniques:

Row 1: Take heavy yarn (HY) or strands of yarn held together (to be about ½″ thick) in your hand. Then with a medium-weight yarn (MY), sc over HY, (about 1″ from end), ch 2, skip a space about 1″, sc over HY, again. Continue in this manner working ch 2, skip a space, sc over HY until your piece measures 42″ (38″) long, ending with a sc. Ch 1, turn. (Ch 1 does not count as a st.)

Row 2 (right side): Bring HY around, and holding it against the row just worked (making sure MY is behind it), crochet over HY into first sc, * ch 2, working over HY, sc in next sc. Rep from * across row. Ch 1, turn.

Rep Row 2 until border measures about 4″ from beg. Fasten off.

BODY PATTERNS:

Row 1: With right side facing you, work 84 (76) sc as evenly as possible over ch 2 sps of last row. Ch 1, turn if you wish to change color leaving about a 3″ end.

The remainder of this garment is done entirely in single crochet stitches and an original stitch called "Overlay St."

When I used the single crochet stitch I worked in *both loops* of the stitch on some rows and in either the *front* or *back* lp of the st on other rows for a variety of texture.

Overlay St:

Row 1: With right side of work facing you, sc in *back lp* of each st across row. Fasten off. Do not turn.

Row 2: Rep last row once more.

Overlay St Row: With right side facing you, sc in front lp of first sc of Row 1, ch 2, skip first sc of Row 2, sc in front lp of next sc of Row 2, * ch 2, sc in front lp of next sc of Row 1, ch 2, sc in front lp of next sc of Row 2. Rep from * across. Fasten off. Continue to work in desired pattern of single crochet and overlay stitch until jacket measures about 22″, (19″) from beginning or desired length to under arm ending on a wrong side row.

To Divide for Fronts and Back:

RIGHT FRONT:

With right side of work facing you, work in desired pattern across first 19 (16) sts. Continue until piece measures 7½″ (6″) from beg, ending at front edge.

To Shape Neck: Skip first 4 (3) sts at beg of row, work in pattern to end of row.

To Dec 1 Sc: Draw up a lp in each of 2 sts, yo, draw through both lps on hook (1 sc dec). Dec 1 st at front edge every row three times. 12 (10) sts remain. Work even if necessary until arm hole measures 9½″ (8″) from beg. Fasten off.

BACK:

Go back to original dividing row. With right side facing you, skip next 4 (6) sts for under arm. Work in pattern across next 38 (32) sts. Continue to work on these sts until back measures 1 row less than front. Work across first 12 (10) sts. Fasten off. Skip next 14 (12) sts for back of neck. Work across remaining 12 (10) sts for other shoulder. Fasten off.

LEFT FRONT:

Go back to original dividing row. With right side facing you, skip next 4 (6) sts for under arm. Work across remaining 19 (16) sts to correspond to right front reversing all shaping. Sew shoulder seams.

SLEEVES:

The sleeves of the original garment were done entirely in single crochet. You may wish to do the same. The sleeves are best worked from the top down. It is important that they fit properly into the armhole. I advise you to work for about 1″ in desired pattern; fold sleeve in half, placing chain edge against arm edge to make sure pieces are flush.

Row 1: Work a chain to measure about 19″ (16″). Work in desired pattern until sleeve measures 20″ (18″) from beg or desired length to under arm. Fasten off.

Front Edging: Work 2 rows of sc along each front to measure about ¾″, making sure work lies flat and there are the same number of sc along each front edge as evenly spaced as possible.

Next Row: Work a row of sc along front and neck edges.

Following Row: Work a row of reverse sc in each st of last row by working st from left to right. Fasten off.

Belt: Work a chain of about 50″ or desired length. Fasten off.

Finishing: Sew in sleeves. Sew sleeve seams.

Scarf

With desired colors and yarns make a chain to measure about 48″, allowing for fringes at each end.

Row 1: Sc in 2nd ch from hook and in each ch across.

Note: The original scarf was made with rows of half double crochet and single crochet. If you wish to use same color on next row and are working a hdc now you must ch 2 at end of previous row. Ch 2 does not count as a st.

Work in desired pattern until scarf measures about 7″ wide or desired width. Fasten off.

Fringes: Place fringes along each narrow end.

Shopping Bag

Size:

Bag measures approx 15″ × 16″.

Materials:

Medium-weight cotton in 14 different colors, 1 oz. each:
Medium Orange (A)
Medium Blue-Green (B)
Pink (C)
Dark Rose (D)
Purple (E)
Gold (F)
Pale Mauve (G)
Dark Moss Green (H)
Wine (I)
Lavender (J)
Light Moss Green (K)
Light Orange (L)
Dark Blue-Green (M)
Dark Orange (N)

Two ½″-thick, 8″-long dowels.

Hook:

Size C aluminum or size to obtain gauge.

Gauge:

3 sc + 3 ch 1 = 1″.

Note: Since your bag does not have to fit anyone, you can be more flexible with your gauge. Remember, however, that if you get more stitches per inch than specified in the gauge your bag will be that much smaller. If you get fewer stitiches per inch, your bag will be that much longer.
The yarns I used for this project were hand-dyed with chemical dyes that work well on natural fibers such as cotton. Many of

the yarns were colored to begin with and redyed to achieve an interesting variation of the original color or produce an entirely new color. You may desire to explore this technique as well or use what you already have on hand. Starting at lower edge of bag with A, chain 176 to measure about 30″. Sl st to first ch, being careful not to twist work.

Round 1: Ch 1, sc in same place as sl st (place safety pin in sc to mark beg of rnd), * ch 1, skip next ch, sc in next ch. Rep from * ending ch 1, skip last ch. Join with sl st to first sc.

Note: Always mark first st of rnd. Sl st does not count as a st. It is used for joining purposes only.

Round 2: Ch 2 (count 2nd ch as first st of rnd), skip first sc, sc over next ch 1 sp. Rep from * around. Join with sl st to first ch. Fasten off A, leaving a 3″ end.

Round 3: With B, make a lp on hook. Draw up a lp over first st (2nd ch) of last end (2 lps on hook), yo, draw through both lps (sc completed), * ch 1, skip next sc, sc over next ch 1 sp. Rep from * ending ch 1, skip last sc. Join with sl st to first sc.

Round 4: Rep Rnd 2. Fasten off B.

Round 5: With C, rep Rnd 3.

Round 6: Rep Rnd 2. Fasten off C.

Rounds 7 and 8: With D, rep Rnds 3 and 2.

Round 9 (Popcorn Round): With E, make lp on hook, work in pattern across first 4 sts, work over next ch 1 sp in popcorn st as follows: * work 5 dc over ch 1 sp, drop lp from hook, insert hook in both lps of first dc and dropped lp, draw dropped lp through first dc, ch 1 (popcorn made), ch 1, skip next sc, (sc over next ch 1 sp, ch 1, skip next sc) three times. Rep from * across working last rep as follows: work popcorn, ch 1, skip next sc, sc over next ch 1 sp, ch 1, skip last sc. Join.

Round 10: Work in pattern as established, working a ch 1 over each popcorn st. Join. Fasten off E.

Round 11: With A, work in pattern to within ch 1 directly over popcorn st, work on sc over this ch 1 into the center of the popcorn st. Continue in this manner around.

Round 12: Work in pattern as established, working a ch 1 over each sc and a sc over each ch 1. Fasten off.

Rounds 13 and 14: With B, rep Rnds 9 and 10.

Rounds 15 and 16: With F, rep Rnds 11 and 12.

Rounds 17 and 18: With D, rep Rnds 9 and 10.

Rounds 19 and 20: With C, rep Rnds 11 and 12.

Rounds 21 through 28: Rep Rnds 3 and 2, working 2 rnds each G, H, A, and F.

Rounds 29 through 40: Rep Rnds 9 through 12 three times, working 2 rnds each B, G, I, J, K, and D.

Rounds 41 through 48: Rep Rnds 3 and 2, working 2 rnds each C, I, G, and A.

Rounds 49 through 60: Rep Rnds 9 through 12 three times, working 2 rnds each E, F, H, L, A, and M.

Continue in this pattern working 2 rnds each of the following colors: K, D, J, F, M, C, N, H, J, L, I, G, A, M, F, D, E, K, I, L, M, and G. Fasten off.

Note: Marked st at beg of rnd forms center back seam of bag.

CASING FOR DOWEL:

Row 1: With desired color make lp on hook (make sure seam is at center back), sc in first ch 1 sp about ½″ in from side edge,* ch 1, skip next sc, sc in next sp. Rep from * across, ending with a sc about ½″ in from other side edge. Turn.

Row 2: Work a sc over each ch 1 sp and sc across. Ch 1, turn.

Row 3: Sc in each sc across. Ch 1, turn.

Rep Row 3 until casing measures about 1″ from beg. Fasten off. Fold casing over to wrong side of bag and stitch in place along *chain edge only.* Work casing for other side of bag in same way. Insert a dowel in narrow opening of each casing, centering it.

HANDLES:

With desired color, work a chain to measure about 17″ long. Original bag handles were made with one each in B and L.

Row 1: Sc in 2nd ch from hook and in each ch across. Ch 1, turn.

Row 2: Sc in each sc across. Ch 1, turn. Rep Row 2 until piece measures 2″ from beg. Fasten off.

Fold piece in half, then matching opposite side of each stitch of starting chain and each single crochet of last row worked, sl st in each st across, working through both sc sts and ch sts rather tightly so that piece slightly curves. Fasten off. Work another handle in same manner. Stitch each narrow end of handle to lower edge of casing, following photo for placement. Sew bottom.

Barbara Muccio

Barbara Muccio is a completely self-taught craftsperson, and her work is evidence enough that she harbors very few preconceptions about what can be done with what. Her very unusual projects have appeared in Woman's Day, McCall's Needlework & Crafts, Good Housekeeping, *and* Seventeen. *Her work is also often seen in* Coats & Clark *instruction books. Barbara's book credits include* The Best of Woman's Day Crochet, Gloria Vanderbilt Designs For Your Home, The McCall's Book of America's Favorite Needlework & Crafts, The Woman's Day Book of Weekend Crafts, Step-by-Step Flower Craft, *and* Hard Crochet.

"I like experimenting with all sorts of materials. I become enthusiastic about the quality of things—a fiber's color or its sheen, its texture or its body. The character and the particular beauty of each material stimulate ideas. I especially like to use materials in an unexpected way or to work with materials that were not originally meant for the crochet hook. For example, when I see a coil of electrical wire I also see in my mind's eye how beautiful it would look crocheted into a basket.

"I love the challenge of using the useless, of recycling. Pennies flattened on the railroad tracks are fun worked into a necklace; an old ornately carved bone chess piece makes an amusing tassel at the bottom of a little crocheted purse; a lump of green beach grass becomes the knob on a basket cover. In each case, the idea is generated by the interesting oddity.

"In designing projects for magazines or books, I always have the reader in mind. I try to keep the designs as functional, as inexpensive, and as easy to make as possible because I want people to enjoy making them.

"When I create an object from a simple thread, a ball of twine, a spool of wire, I please myself. I have a sense of fulfillment. May all of you who crochet—men, women, and children—have the same wonderful experience!"

Barbara Muccio

Abbreviations, Explanations

Note: "Slip loop" (sl lp) is what I call the knotless loop into which I crochet to begin working in a circle. Its virtues are the lack of a lumpy knot, of particular value with heavy fibers, and the fact that you can draw the center hole tightly closed by pulling on the tail cord.

To make a slip loop, hold cord in left hand just as you do when ready to crochet. With right hand, loop the end cord counterclockwise behind the working cord, with the tail hanging down. Hold the loop with your left thumb and middle finger.

To crochet into the slip loop, insert hook into loop, yarn over hook and draw a loop through to front of slip loop. Chain 1. I call this procedure "make a sl lp and ch 2 up from lp." You are now ready to crochet into the ring, working around both cords.

Cable Cotton
Rope Designs

General Notes:

One-quarter-inch cotton cable rope is put up in 10-lb. tubes, but since the weight may vary somewhat from one tube to another, be sure to specify that you need 10 lbs. minimum weight. That amount will accommodate the three following designs.

Before starting to work, bind the cut ends of the rope with masking tape to avoid ravelling.

While working, always pull slip stitches snugly at the ends of rounds to avoid noticeable bumps. If you wish, work with an old kid glove on your left hand; this will protect sensitive skin. But make sure the glove is white; otherwise you may inadvertently dye the rope.

Use a lot of hook-twisting to help pull the cord through snug stitches.

To fasten off the cord, untwist into three sections and work the ends into existing stitches.

Hang-up

Size:

24" high.

Materials:

2 lbs. (30 yds.) White ¼" cable cotton rope.

Hook:

Size S (19.05 mm) plastic Jiffy.

Round 1: Make a sl lp on hook 18" from end of rope. Ch 2 up from ring. 6 Sc in ring, working around 2 cords. Sl st into beg ch 2 to end rnd. Pull end of cord to tighten ring and draw end down through center hole.

Round 2: 1 Ch, sc 2 in sm pl. 2 Sc in each st to end of rnd. Sl st under 1 cord only of beg to end rnd.

Rounds 3 through 6: Ch 1. Working under 1 outer cord of previous rnd, 1 sc in sm pl. Sc even to end of rnd. Sl st under 1 outer cord of beg ch 1.

Border: Remove hook from lp. Draw lp through same st to outside of work. Sl st 12 sts even around outside edge under 1 cord.

HANDLE:

Ch 10 tightly, drawing each ch back with your hand and forward again with the hook so as to achieve a very tight chain stitch. Skip 2 sts and sl st under 2 cords of the 4th st (going clockwise just as the border went) of border. Cut cord, leaving a 6" end and tie off.

TASSEL:

Cut five 28" lengths and one 12" length of rope. Fold each of the 28" lengths in half and draw each one up through the bottom hole of the hang-up. Tie all tog with the 12" length. Trim ends of knot and pull the 10 ends all the way back down. Untwist each end into 3 separate sections. Fringe the bottom 2" of each of these 30 ends. Trim if necessary.

Insert a 12-oz. plastic frozen juice container in hang-up if you wish to use it for fresh flowers or ivy. Or fill it with a dried flower arrangement or with wooden spoons for the kitchen.

Oval Basket

Size:

9½″ high × 11½″ long.

Materials:

Slightly under 4 lbs. (58 yds.) White ¼″ cable cotton rope.

Hook:

Size S (19.05 mm) plastic Jiffy.

Note: Basket should be worked tightly throughout.

Round 1: Make a sl lp on hook 12″ from end of rope. Ch 2 up from lp. 8 Sc in lp around both cords. Sl st into top of beg ch 2 to close rnd. Pull end of cord as tight as possible.

Round 2: Ch 1, sc 2 in sm pl. Hdc and dc in next st. Dc and hdc in next st. 2 Sc in next st. 2 Sc in next st. Hdc and dc in next st. Dc and hdc in next st. 2 Sc in next st. Sl st in beg ch 1.

Round 3: Ch 1, 2 sc in sm pl. * 2 Sc in next st. 1 Hdc in next st. 2 Dc in next st. 2 Dc in next st. 1 Hdc in next st. 2 Sc in next st. 2 Sc in next st. Rep from * two times. Sl st in back cord of beg ch 1.

Round 4: Ch 1. Turn work. 1 Sc in back cord in same place. Work rest of rnd in outer cord only, with "wrong" side facing you. Sc even to end of rnd. Sl st in 1 inner cord of beg ch 1.

Round 5: Ch 1. Turn work. 1 Sc in 1 outer cord in same place. Work rest of rnd in outer cord only with "right" side facing you. Sc even to end of rnd. Sl st in 1 inner cord of beg ch 1.

Round 6: Ch 1. Do not turn work. 1 Sc in sm pl, sc even to end of rnd, working under 2 cords throughout. Sl st in outer cord of beg ch 1.

Round 7 (Handle): Ch 12. Turning ch so that the bumpy side faces up, sl st into outer cord of the 14th st around edge of basket. Sl st back along the 12 ch, working around two cords of ch. (Working cord will be above handle and hook will be underneath.) Sl st into edge of basket at beg of handle.

Round 8 (Border): Sl st around inner edge of basket in 1 inner cord, working from *inside* of basket. Cut cord and tie off.

Vase

Size:

10″ high, 10″ in diameter at top, 10″ at base.

Materials:

4 lbs. (61 yds.) ¼″ White cable cotton rope.

Hook:

Size S (19.05 mm) plastic Jiffy.

Round 1: Make a sl lp on hook 12″ from end of rope. Ch 2 up from lp. 8 Sc in lp around 1 cord only. Sl st in beg ch 1 to close rnd. Pull end of cord as tight as possible.

Round 2: Ch 1, 2 sc in sm pl, 2 sc even around. Sl st in beg ch 1.

Round 3: Ch 1. Sl st even around, down through 2 cords, to form edge of base.

Round 4: Remove hook from lp. Draw lp through to back of work and sl st. Proceeding on "wrong" side of work now, and from outer edge of circle toward inside, ch 2; * 1 sc in next st, in 1 outer cord rep from * all around. Sl st into top of beg ch 2 to end rnd. Tie off beginning cord end.

Rounds 5 through 9: Ch 1, 1 sc sm pl. 16 Sc even around. Sl st in beg ch 1 to end rnd.

Round 10: Ch 1, 1 sc in sm pl. 2 Sc even. Inc 1 in next (4th) st. * 3 Sc even, inc 1 in next st rep from * three times. Sl st in beg ch 1.

*Round 11: Ch 1, 1 sc in sm pl, 1 sc in next st. Inc 1 st in next st. * 4 Sc even, inc 1 st in next st, rep from * 3 times. 2 Sc even. Sl st in beg ch 1 to end rnd.

Cut cord, leaving a 12″ end. Tie off.

Note: To use vase for dried flower arrangements, insert a sand-filled coffee can that has been painted white; or for a planter, fill coffee can, painted white, with dirt and desired plant and insert. For fresh flowers, a mayonnaise or pickle jar will do.

Striped Basket
with Cover

Size:

11½″ tall, 11½″ diameter at top, 14″ diameter of base.

Materials:

Three 280-foot tubes of light color ⁵⁄₃₂″ jute welt cord (A).
Three 280-foot tubes of dark color, ⁵⁄₃₂″ jute welt cord (B).

Hooks:

Sizes N and K (for fastening off ends), aluminum.
This basket is worked in a spiral with no separate rounds. Mark the beginning of the first dark color round; that single mark, along with the natural color pattern progression, will identify the rounds with no further marking.
Cord will kink up periodically, so untwist it by letting work hang down and untwist itself. Leave hook in place in a stitch so as to lock work into place and avoid ravelling.
When dropping or picking up colors, always move cord to front or back of work in the same way each time to avoid tangling; for instance, dark cord always to the front.
To change color: With two loops on hook in last stitch of old color, draw new color through loops on hook, completing the sc. To carry unused color along, sc around it as you go.
Crochet snugly to give all possible body to this basket.

Note: Basket is worked with right side facing you.
Round 1: With A, make a sl lp with 10″ tail, ch 2 up from lp and 8 sc in lp around the two cords.
Round 2: * With B, 2 sc in next st; with A, 2 sc in next st, rep from * four times. Tighten beg tail and tie off. Mark beg of Rnd 2.

Follow color pattern as established throughout rest of basket:

Round 3: * 2 Sc in next st, 1 sc in next st, rep from * eight times (one time in each color section).

Round 4: * 2 Sc in next st, 2 sc even, rep from * eight times (one time in each color section).

Round 5: * 2 Sc in next st, 3 sc even, rep from * eight times (one time in each color section).

Round 6: * 2 Sc in next st, 4 sc even, rep from * eight times (one time in each color section).

Round 7: * 2 Sc in next st, 5 sc even, rep from * eight times (one time in each color section).

Round 8: * Sc even, changing color of 4th st in each color section, rep from * eight times.

Round 9: * 2 Sc in next st, sc 1 in next st, 2 sc in next st, 1 sc in next st, 2 sc in next st, sc 1 in next st, 2 sc in next st, rep from * eight times, being sure to follow color change from previous rnd.

Round 10: Sc even around.

Round 11: * Dec 1 in next 2 sts, 1 sc in next st, dec 1 in next 2 sts, 1 sc in next st, dec 1 in next 2 sts, 1 sc in next st, dec 1 in next 2 sts, rep from * eight times.

Rounds 12 through 22: Sc even.

Begin to define rnds now. To do this, at end of next rnd, sl st into first sc of previous rnd, ch 1, and make first st of present rnd in the same place as the sl st and ch 1.

Rounds 23 through 25: Sc even.

Round 26:

Edge: Continue with A for one more st with a sl st into next st, thereby making four A sts instead of three, breaking the pattern. With A lp on hook, sl st with B into next (B) sc of previous rnd. Sl st the rest of this rnd following the color pattern but working one stitch forward of it. This will give an even look to the finished edge. Work alternately over and under the cords being carried along so as to work them into back of stitches as you proceed. End off in pattern: After last three A sts, cut cords and draw B cord through to front and through the A lp on hook. Then draw A to inside of work through next B st. Fasten off both cords, weaving ends neatly into work.

BASKET COVER:

Work same as Basket through Round 12, except that Rounds 10, 11, and 12 should be defined. Work last round of cover same as Round 26 of Basket.

With A, make a sl lp with 12″ tail, ch 2 up from lp and 6 sc in lp around both cords. Pull tail tight. 6 Sc even. * Skip 1 st and draw up lp under both cords in next st, rep from * two times. Cut cord with a 12″ tail and draw it through the 3 lps on hook. Draw this cord through knob to opposite side of bottom from the first tail. Use the two ends to tie knob onto cover, drawing cords through cover at outside of first rnd, not in center hole.

STRIPED WALL ORNAMENT OR BOWL:

Work same as Basket through Round 11, except Rounds 10 and 11 should be defined.

Round 12: Same as Round 26 of Basket, except do not fasten off B.

Round 13: With B, sl st around outside of edge, just under previous round. Fasten off.

Pillow

Size:

Pillow front is about 17½″ long by 17¼″ wide.

Materials:

Wool needle.
16″ × 16″ pillow.

(A)—1 lb. White imported natural unscoured wool, spun thick and thin, approx 250 yds. per lb.
(B)—2 skeins White imported mountain sheep's wool, 3⅜ oz. each.
(C)—1 skein Medium Brown imported mountain sheep's wool, 3⅜ oz.
(D)—15 ft. of wool roving.
(E)—6 ft. of jute roving.

Hook:

Size N aluminum or size to obtain gauge.

Gauge:

5 sts = 3″. This is uneven work, so the gauge is approximate.
Pillow is worked with two cords held together and is worked into *top two cords only* of previous row throughout. It is done entirely in slip stitch except for the seven textured rows, which are done in single crochet over the filler material.
Pillow is made as a long rectangle, half with textured rows and half without, and it is folded in half and sewn together over a pillow form.
Give all fillers a 3″ tail at beginning and end of rows.

Note: Roll the skein of C into two equal-sized balls.

FRONT:

Row 1: With A and B tog, ch 30 and sl st 29 sts back along ch in top two cords only.
Row 2: Ch 1, turn work, sl st 29 sts even.
Row 3: Rep Row 2.

Row 4: Taking up filler material E, lay it across work between the working cord and the loop on hook. Ch 1 around filler. Turn work and * 2 sc even over filler, 1 sc in next st under filler, moving it aside as you st, leaving it exposed, rep from * across row, ending 2 sc even. Cut filler. (Working over the jute roving may cause this row to stretch somewhat. If it does, gently push stitches together a bit as you tighten the filler.)

Rows 5, 6, and 7: Rep Row 2.

Rows 8 and 9: Drop A and B. Attach two strands of C and rep Row 2. Drop C and pick up A and B.

Row 10: Taking up filler material D, lay it across work between the working cord and the loop on hook. Ch 1 around filler. Turn work and * 2 sc even over filler; 1 sc in next st under filler, moving it aside as you st, leaving it exposed; then give it a slight twist and a push to puff it out before doing the next st, rep from * across row, ending 2 sc even. Cut filler.

Row 11: Rep Row 2.

Row 12: Rep Row 10.

Row 13: Rep Row 2, then drop A and B.

Rows 14 and 15: Pick up C and Rep Row 2. Then drop C.

Rows 16 through 19: Pick up A and B and rep Row 2.

Row 20: Rep Row 4.

Rows 21 through 23: Rep Row 2. Then drop A and B and pick up C.

Rows 24 and 25: Rep Row 2 with C. Then fasten off C and pick up A and B.

Rows 26 and 27: Rep Row 2 with A and B.

Row 28: Rep Row 10.

Row 29: Rep Row 2.

Row 30: Rep Row 10.

Row 31: Drop A and B. Remove loop from hook and let it just hang there. Draw up loop with C at opposite side of work from where A and B were just dropped. Ch 1 and sl st 29 sts even, working this row in same direction in which it was worked in previous row. Fasten off C.

Row 32: Picking up A and B at point where previous row just ended, draw up existing A and B loop through first stitch in C row; ch 1 and sl st 29 sts even.

Rows 33 and 34: Rep Row 2.

Row 35: Rep Row 4.

Rows 36 and 37: Rep Row 2.

PILLOW BACK:

Mark beginning of back at both ends of first row. Also mark beginning and end of another row about 8″ farther along into work to facilitate positioning sides evenly when sewing together.

Roll up pillow front, facing in, and tie it in two places, drawing ties through the work and around the roll; it will be easier to use this way.

Continuing with A and B, rep Row 2 for 44 more rows. Fasten off.

PUTTING TOGETHER:

Sew front and back together right side out with a single strand of A, beginning at center fold of work at the point where you marked the beginning of pillow back. Sew sides together in the two outer horizontal cords of each edge. As the rows are not even on front and back, you must ease the extra back rows into the front. Do this in the same way you would decrease stitches, by sewing two back rows into one front row. The row you marked in middle of back will help you position work evenly.

Sew lengthwise ends tog; then position crochet on pillow form and sew other side up to center fold, easing back into front as before. Fasten off.

Mirror with Rope
Frame and Ruffles

Size:

19″ diameter.

Materials:

⅛″-thick round mirror, 14″ diameter.
2 pieces corrugated cardboard, 14″ diameter.
103 yds. (1¾ lbs.) ⁵⁄₃₂″ jute welt cord, Natural color.
3 balls ¹⁄₁₆″ jute wrapping twine, ½ lb. each.
1 100-yd. ball ¹⁄₁₆″ 4-ply Brown crochet cotton.

Hooks:

Size 16 wood afghan.
Sizes K and 9 aluminum.

Note: Work snugly through Round 14 in order to give all possible firmness to jute welt cord.

BACK OF FRAME:

Round 1: Make a sl lp on 16 wood hook with ⁵⁄₃₂″ jute welt cord. Ch 2 up from lp. Working around two cords (loop cord and end of cord), 7 sc in lp. Sl st into beg ch 1 to close rnd. Pull end of cord tight and tie off.

Round 2: Ch 1, 1 sc in sm pl. 2 Sc in each st around. Sl st in beg ch 1 to close rnd.

Round 3: Ch 1, 1 sc in sm pl. * 2 Sc in next st, 1 sc in next st, rep from * to end. Sl st in beg ch 1.

Round 4: Ch 1, 1 sc in sm pl. * 2 Sc in next st, 2 sc even, rep from * to end. Sl st in beg ch 1.

Round 5: Ch 1, 1 sc in sm pl. * 2 Sc in next st, 3 sc even, rep from * to end. Sl st in beg ch 1.

Round 6: Ch 1, 1 sc in sm pl. * 2 Sc in next st, 4 sc even, rep from * to end. Sl st in beg ch 1. (Your circle should measure 9″ in diameter.)

Round 7: Ch 1, 1 sc in sm pl. * 2 Sc in next st, 5 sc even, rep from * to end. Sl st in beg ch 1.

Round 8: Ch 1, 1 sc in sm pl. * 2 Sc in next st, 6 sc even, rep from * to end. Sl st in beg ch 1.

Round 9: Ch 1, 1 sc in sm pl. * 2 Sc in next st, 7 sc even, rep from * to end, Sl st in beg ch 1.

Round 10: Ch 1, 1 sc in sm pl. * 2 Sc in next st, 8 sc even, rep from * to end. Sl st in beg ch 1.

Round 11: Ch 1, 1 sc in sm pl. * 2 Sc in next st, 9 sc even, rep from * to end. Sl st in beg ch 1.

(Your circle should measure 15½″ in diameter.)

EDGE OF FRAME:

Round 12: Working under one inner cord throughout this rnd, ch 1, 1 sc in sm pl. Sc even to end. Sl st under both cords of beg ch 1.

INNER EDGE OF FRAME:

Round 13: Rep Rnd 12. Insert corrugated cardboard circles and mirror into frame.

Round 14: Draw up long lp. Remove hook from lp. From outside of frame edge, insert hook into beg ch 1 of previous rnd and pull lp through. Tighten lp if necessary. You are now in position to work clockwise around frame, facing toward inside. Crossing hook over working cord, *snugly* sl st under 1 cord of each st to end of rnd; cut cord and tie off.

HANG-UP LOOP:

Cut a 24″ piece of cord and tie on a hang-up lp in back of mirror about 2″ from top.

RUFFLE:

Round 1: Working with three cords together, make a sl knot with the ⅟₁₆″ jute wrapping twine. With #16 hook and with mirror facing you, draw lp through one cord at back edge of frame and ch 1. 2 Sc in sm pl. 2 Sc in each st around back outside edge. Sl st in beg ch 1 to end rnd.

Round 2: With K hook, ch 4. 3 Tr in sm pl. 4 Tr in each st around. Sl st in top of beg ch 4 to close rnd. Cut cords and tie off.

RUFFLE EDGING:

With Brown crochet cotton, make a sl knot. Draw lp through top of a tr using the #9 hook. Ch 1, 2 sc in sm pl. 2 Sc in each st around. Cut cord and end off.

Arrange ruffles symmetrically as shown. Press ruffles slightly inward toward mirror all around.

Lampshade

Size:

18″ high, 14″ in diameter.

Materials:

½ lb. wool roving.

1 skein White imported mountain sheep's wool, 3⅜ ozs.

1 skein Charcoal Brown imported mountain sheep's wool, 3⅜ ozs.

1 lb. White imported natural unscoured wool, spun thick and thin, approx 250 yds. per lb.

1 lampshade top-frame, 14″ diameter.

1 lampshade bottom ring, 14″ diameter.

Hooks:

Size K aluminum.

Size 13 wood afghan.

Plastic Jiffy hook size Q (15.90 mm)

Materials needed to electrify as a hanging lamp:

150-watt coated globe bulb.

Porcelain socket with pull chain.

⅜″ Threaded steel pipe 1″ long.

Hexagonal nut.

Round white electrical wire, as needed.

Note: 3 sc = 1″ on rim of frame. Work snugly. Keep shade turned inside out as you proceed. All work takes place on inside of frame up until last rnd.

Round 1: Make sl st on K hook with White sheep's wool. Working around both the top frame and the wool roving tog, snugly work 132 sc around rim. Sl st into beg sc to end rnd.

Round 2: Ch 1. Working snugly over roving with White sheep's wool, 1 sc in sm pl. 2 Sc even. Throw roving over to outside of frame and 2 sc even under the roving. Bump: Giving roving a slight twist and a push to puff it up a bit, 1 sc over roving into next st. Bump completed. Pattern: * 3 Sc even over roving, 2 sc even under roving bump; sc over roving into next st, rep from * twenty times, ending 3 sc even over roving 2 sc even under roving, 1 sc in next st. Draw roving *toward* you to carry it along on inside of work. Sl st into beg ch 1 to end rnd.

Round 3: Do not work over roving in this rnd.
With Brown, ch 1, 1 hdc in sm pl, hdc even to end of rnd, sl st in beg ch 1. Drop Brown.

Round 4: With White sheep's wool, repeat Rnd 2. Drop White. Fasten roving off.

Round 5: With Brown, rep Rnd 3.

Round 6: With #13 wood hook and Brown, ch 1, dec 1 in sm pl and next st. * Dec 1 sc in next 2 sts, rep from * to end of rnd, ending sl st in beg ch 1. Fasten off Brown.

Rounds 7 through 24: With Q hook and White unscoured thick-and-thin wool, ch 1, 1 sc in sm pl, sc even to end of rnd. Sl st in beg ch 1 to end rnd. Fasten off.

Round 25: With #13 hook and Brown, ch 1, sc 1 in sm pl, sc even to end of rnd, sl st in beg ch 1.

Round 26: With K hook and Brown, 1 ch, 1 hdc in sm pl, 2 hdc in each st to end of rnd, sl st in beg ch 1. Drop Brown.

Round 27: With K hook, White sheep's wool and roving, rep Rnd 2. Drop White sheep's wool and roving.

Round 28: With K hook and Brown, rep Rnd 3. Fasten off Brown.

Round 29: With K hook, White sheep's wool and roving, rep Rnd 2.

Round 30: *Turn shade right side out before beginning last rnd.* With K hook and White sheep's wool, ch 1 around bottom lampshade ring. Working snugly over ring and roving, 132 sc even around ring. Sl st and fasten off.

Appendix

The following is a list of projects in which special or unusual yarns were used. Yarns noted are not necessarily the only ones used in the projects mentioned.

Lillian Bailey

Mohair Pastel Blouson with V–Neck (page 4):

Stanley Berroco Dji Dji variegated brushed wool, 77 percent wool–23 percent nylon.

Impressionist Garden Coat (page 9):

Stanley Berroco Dji Dji variegated brushed wool, 77 percent wool–23 percent nylon.

Donegal Tweed Suit (page 13):

Tahki Donegal Tweed homespun, bulky weight and worsted weight; Stanley Berroco variegated brushed wool, 77 percent wool–23 percent nylon.

Alpaca Coat (page 18):

Plymouth Indiecita alpaca, worsted weight; Stanley Berroco Que Linda variegated loop yarn, 95 percent wool–5 percent nylon.

Pot Pourri Jacket (page 23):

Reynolds Velourette cotton viscose chenille; Stanley Berroco Dji Dji variegated brushed wool, 77 percent wool–23 percent nylon.

Linda Osborne Blood

Afghan Stitch Vest (page 35):

Bernat Mohair Plus; Joseph Galler Majestic Mohair; Stanley Berroco Dji Dji brushed wool, medium to heavyweight.

Basketweave Hooded Jacket (page 40):	Tahki Donegal Tweed homespun, medium weight.
Jacket and Skirt Set (page 53):	Tahki Donegal Tweed homespun, medium weight; Stanley Berroco Dji Dji brushed wool, medium to heavyweight.

Nan Jennes Brown

Mayan Figure Coat (page 62):	Tahki Donegal Tweed homespun, worsted weight; Stanley Berroco brushed wool, 70 percent wool–30 percent viscose.
Large Victorian Pouch (page 71):	Lilly Double Quick 8-cord cable-twist mercerized crochet cotton.
Woman's Textured Top (page 76):	Reynolds Ruban–Rayonne woven edge ribbon; Stanley Berroco brushed wool, 70 percent wool–30 percent viscose.

Judith Copeland

Striped Pullover (page 93):	William Unger Scheepjes Natuurwol, sport weight.
Bulky Yarn Pullover (page 96):	Reynolds Lopi 100 percent wool, bulky weight.
Mixed Yarn Pullover (page 98):	Plymouth Indiecita alpaca, lightweight.
Mittens (page 105):	Plymouth Indiecita alpaca, lightweight.
Hat (page 107):	William Unger Rygja wool, bulky weight.

Del Pitt Feldman

Fantasy Coat (page 117):	Reynold Welcomme Pernelle, 85 percent wool–15 percent synthetic.

Arlene Mintzer

Capelet and Skirt (pages 172 and 176):	Tahki Donegal Tweed homespun, medium weight; Tahki Designer homespun tweed, medium weight; Joseph Galler Majestic Mohair; Joseph Galler Persian cotton.

Popcorn Vest (page 179):

Tahki Donegal Tweed homespun, worsted weight; Bucilla Persian-type needle-point and crewel yarn.

Man's or Woman's Long Jacket and Scarf (pages 184 and 188):

Tahki Donegal Tweed homespun, super-heavyweight; Manos del Uruguay hand-spun and hand-dyed variegated wool, worsted-weight; Plymouth Indiecita alpaca, medium weight; Stanley Berroco Que Linda variegated loop yarn, 95 percent wool–5 percent nylon; Stanley Berroco Zoom Zoom, 60 percent viscose–40 percent wool.

Shopping Bag (page 189):

Lilly Double Quick 8-cord cable-twist mercerized crochet cotton.

Barbara Muccio

Pillow (page 206):

Reynolds Lopi 100 percent wool, bulky weight; Tsunami natural, unscoured wool, spun thick and thin, from Coulter Studios. Wool roving and jute roving from Coulter Studios.

Mirror with Rope Frame and Ruffles (page 210):

Coats & Clark Speed-Cro-Sheen 4-ply brown crochet cotton.

Lampshade (page 214):

Reynolds Lopi 100 percent wool, bulky weight; Tsunami natural, unscoured wool, spun thick and thin, from Coulter Studios.

Sources

Belding Lilly Co.
Lilly Mills
Shelby, NC 28150

Emile Bernat & Sons, Inc.
230 Fifth Avenue
New York, NY 10001

Stanley Berroco, Inc.
140 Mendon Street
Uxbridge, MA 10569

Bucilla Yarn Co.
30–20 Thompson Avenue
Long Island City, NY 11101

Coats & Clark, Inc.
75 Rockefeller Plaza
New York, NY 10019

Coulter Studios
118 East 59th Street
New York, NY 10022

Coyote
Box 2159
GPO New York, NY 10001

Joseph Galler, Inc.
149 Fifth Avenue
New York, NY 10001

Manos del Uruguay
366 Fifth Avenue
New York, NY 10001

Plymouth Yarn Co.
Box 28
Bristol, PA 19007

Reynold Yarns, Inc.
15 Ozer Avenue
Hauppauge, NY 11787

Tahki Imports
62 Madison Street
Hackensack, NJ 07601

William Unger & Co., Inc.
230 Fifth Avenue
New York, NY 10001